Butterflies and Lizards, Beryl and Me

Ruth Lercher Bornstein

MARSHALL CAVENDISH • NEW YORK

I want to thank the many friends and colleagues who have given me their generous critiques and encouragement through the years. A special thanks to Susan Pearson for her invaluable suggestions, to Judy Campbell for her insight, to my agent Susan Cohen and my editor Judith Whipple for their faith in the story, and to Charlotte Zolotow for telling me way back then that what I was writing was a novel.

Marshall Cavendish, 99 White Plains Road, Tarrytown, NY 10591
Library of Congress Cataloging-in-Publication Data

Bornstein, Ruth.
Butterflies and lizards, Beryl and me / by Ruth Lercher Bornstein.
p.   cm.
Summary: In 1936, eleven-year-old Charlotte and her mother move to tiny
Valley Junction, Missouri, where Charlotte befriends an eccentric old woman
in spite of her mother's and others' warnings.
ISBN 0-7614-5118-8
1. Depressions –1929 –Juvenile fiction. [1.Depressions –1929 –Fiction.
2. Eccentrics and eccentricities –Fiction. 3. Interpersonal relations –Fiction.
4. Old age –Fiction. 5. Moving, Household –Fiction. 6. Missouri –Fiction.] I. Title.
PZ7.B64848 Bu 2001   [Fic] –dc21   2001047473

The text of this book is set in 12 point Berthold Baskerville
Printed in the United States of America
First edition
3 5 6 4 2

To the memory of my parents, and the first Beryl

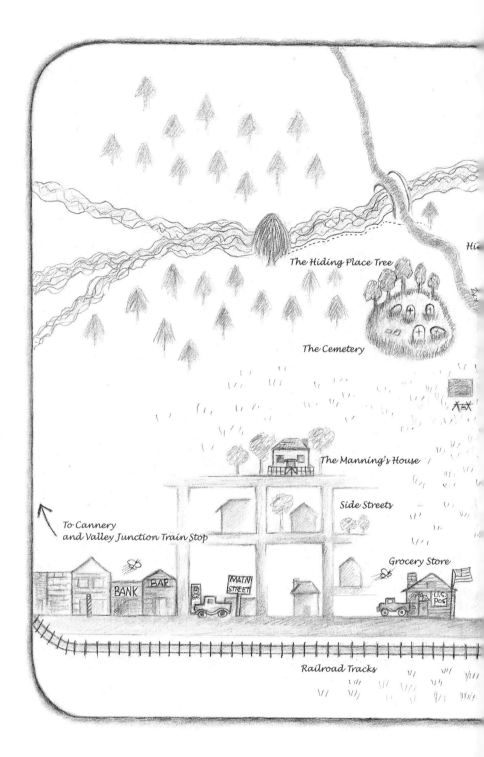

The Hiding Place Tree

Hi

The Cemetery

The Manning's House

Side Streets

To Cannery
and Valley Junction Train Stop

Grocery Store

BANK BAR

MAIN
STREET

U.S.
POST

Railroad Tracks

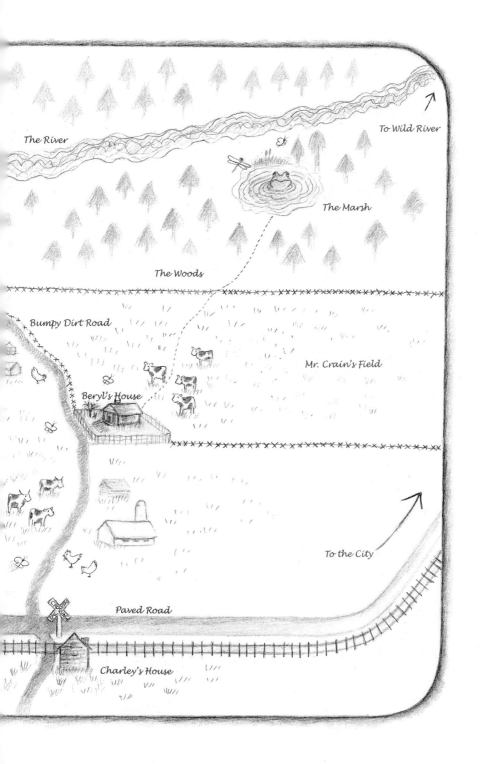

The River

To Wild River

The Marsh

The Woods

Bumpy Dirt Road

Mr. Crain's Field

Beryl's House

To the City

Paved Road

Charley's House

This story takes place when times were hard,
when trains ran between small towns,
and when hobos rode on them.

1
Valley Junction

A piercing whistle jerked me awake; then a rumbling and a rattling as if it was coming through my room. My heart pounded and I grabbed the edges of my cot. The train screeched past.

Downstairs a door slammed. My mother, gone to work. It was her first day at her new job. And my first day in this place called Valley Junction.

I'd always wanted to live in the country, always drawn pictures of grass and trees and big, open sky. But now I wasn't so sure. Now that it was just her and me.

My attic bedroom was already hot and stuffy. I sat up and looked at the rough-planked walls around me. Last night I'd climbed the stairs and claimed this hidden-away room for my own. Now I saw that the window was sealed shut with about a hundred years of paint and I'd suffocate if I didn't leave the door open for air. I wouldn't have complete privacy after all.

I reached under my cot where I'd stored my things and pushed past my box of scrap paper and pencil stubs to get to the suitcase with my clothes. I pulled on shorts and a blouse and clumped down the narrow stairs.

At the bottom was the dark, dingy kitchen. My mother's clock and calendar were already up on the peeling, brown wall. June 10, 1936, was circled with the word, MOVE.

Our card table and two chairs looked lost in the middle of the torn linoleum floor. Our cardboard boxes were stacked by the wall. The jar of peanut butter and box of soda crackers sat on the table.

The clock ticked.

I ran up to my room and dragged out my art box. Armed with paper and a pencil in my pocket, I went downstairs to the kitchen and out the kitchen door.

And there it was. Bigger and wider and bluer than anything I'd ever imagined. And I didn't have to climb to a tenement roof to see it. I wanted to stretch my arms up, wanted to shout, "Hello up there, sky!"

But I didn't. I only stood still and said it to myself. Because it was so quiet. No cars, no streetcars, no people. No other houses on the block. There *was* no block. Just dusty weeds and a bumpy dirt road that went from our house over the railroad tracks and off into the distance.

The tracks marked the end of our dinky dirt yard. A railroad crossing sign stood on the other side, and behind it, going the same way as the tracks, was a road that was paved. Two kids on bikes were turning onto it from the dirt road. They saw me and skidded to a stop. Their bikes were shiny and new.

"Hey!" the boy yelled. "Where'd *you* come from?"

I stepped cautiously over the tracks. The girl looked my age. Her pink blouse and shorts were ironed and starchy clean, and she had huge blue eyes and blond curls. She was almost as pretty as the movie star on my mother's calendar. The blond, freckle-faced boy was younger.

"Hey, I was talking to you," the boy said.

Oh. I cleared my throat. "I just moved here and I–"

"What's your name?"

"Uh–Charley."

"Charley? That's a boy's name."

"I know it." My face heated up. "So what?" I looked at the girl. "What's yours?"

"I'm Mikey Manning," the boy chanted. "My sister's Maxine Manning, my mom's Marjorie Manning, and my dad's Mickey Manning." He giggled. "The four *Ms*. We should be in the movies!"

Maxine punched her brother's arm. "Shut up, Mikey."

I could see the four blond *Ms* around a table with a white tablecloth and lots of food, talking together, laughing–the perfect movie family.

"You'd better know," the boy went on, "that my dad's the most important man around here–he owns just about everything. He was a famous football star at Amesville High School, too. Who's your dad?"

My face got hotter.

They both stood there, straddling their bikes, staring at me.

"He—he's not here now. He's gone. He works."

"What does he do?"

"He . . . he sells things."

"What *kind* of things?"

I was ready this time. "Important things. Like Frigidaires and RCA Victor radios. Things like that."

The boy seemed impressed. But the girl was looking at my run-down sneakers, at my crumpled blouse and my hacked-off hair. "How old are you, anyway?" she asked.

"Twelve," I lied.

"Huh. You don't look that old."

I knew I was skinny—some people might say runty—even for eleven. "Well, I am!" I waited a minute, then asked, "How old are you?"

"Same as you." She held up her arm with its big, gold wristwatch. "It's nine o'clock, Mikey. Let's get going. Mom said we're having pancakes for breakfast."

My mouth watered. The watch gave off glinty sparks.

"Aw, just 'cause Dad gave you his old watch you think you can boss me." Still, the boy hopped on his bike and followed his sister down the paved road.

There were some buildings on it, farther down. The kids turned off somewhere before that. I started walking toward what must be the town of Valley Junction.

In a few minutes I came to a ramshackle grocery store. An American flag and a UNITED STATES POST OFFICE sign hung by the door. I frowned. There wouldn't be any mail for me.

The front of the store was papered over with old signs and posters. There was a jolly, red-cheeked Santa Claus, a grinning clown from a 1930 county fair, a laughing, blond-haired boy biting into a huge slice of watermelon, and a pretty, dimple-faced girl glad to be drinking Coca-Cola. My fingers itched to draw mustaches on them all.

I stared at the picture of the handsome, bare-chested man swinging through the trees.

I knew the movie. *Tarzan the Ape Man.*

I remembered that we came in late. I remembered that it was exactly two years ago.

Daddy gives me a nickel for popcorn, then we run up the stairs to the balcony so he can smoke. Tarzan is just carrying Jane off to his jungle home in the trees. We hold our breath as he swims across a raging river, wrestles crocodiles, and fights lions and leopards. His awesome call gives me the chills. At the end Jane decides to stay with him, and I'm sure they live happily ever after.

We'd missed the cartoon and all the rest so we sit through the newsreel, which shows ladies parading around in the newest summer fashions. Mom would love this part, I think to myself. Then we laugh hard at Mickey Mouse playing music on a cow's teeth. We laugh even harder at Laurel and Hardy. Then we watch Tarzan all over again. When we walk outside, it's dark and the street lights are on.

"I could make movies, too," Daddy says, "if I had a break. If I had the money."

I look up at him. Daddy could be a movie star, too! Next to my dad and my blond-haired, blue-eyed mom I feel very plain— plain brown hair, plain brown eyes, plain face.

I drag Daddy past the five-and-ten. I'd stolen some pencils the day before and I'm still scared I'll be arrested. Like I was once—a policeman had caught me with crayons in my hand and hauled me home by the collar. Daddy thought it was funny, but Mom had one of her screaming fits. Anyway, that didn't stop me. If I can't buy what I need I just have to steal it.

Outside the soup kitchen a scruffy man holds up a sign: WILL TAKE ANY JOB. Something smells good from inside, and I tug at Daddy's hand. But he keeps on walking, his head up, looking straight ahead. "You're going to draw Tarzan now, I bet," he says. "Am I right, Charley?"

I grin. "Right!" Daddy always likes what I draw. And I like that he has a special name for me, too—even if it does sound like a boy's.

"How about making a picture of me as Tarzan? Just for fun."

"Sure! And I'll be Jane. We'll swing through the trees together."

Daddy laughs. "Wouldn't you rather be my little ape friend?"

I laugh, too. "No, I'm going to be Jane." I swing his hand. We're a team, Daddy and me!

At the grocery store Daddy buys a package of Hostess Twinkies. "My last nickel," he says. "For your mother."

I know why he bought the Twinkies. She'd have to be told about Daddy's job.

We creep up our dark stairs. Before we get to the door, Mom flings it open, and she's purple-in-the-face mad.

"Where were you? Do you know what time it is? Charlotte, I told you to stay home while I was at work. I was out of my mind with worry!"

I smell burned potatoes and bacon grease. I hope there's bacon, too.

Daddy tries to give her the package of Twinkies, but she bats it out of his hand. "So that's it!" she yells. "Trying to butter me up because you've lost another job. And you took her out and spent your last dime. You're teaching her to be a no-good dreamer like you!"

Daddy pushes past her. She pulls me in and slams the door shut. She keeps screaming so loud I'm sure everyone in the whole building, the whole block, can hear her.

"I can't take it anymore! I was better off alone. At least I didn't have to support a whole family!"

I run into the other room and stick my fingers in my ears.

2

Butterflies and Bikes

I was still standing there, still staring at the movie poster, when the grocery door opened and hillbilly music spilled out from a radio inside. I stepped away from the picture of Tarzan.

A man with gray-sprinkled hair came out lugging a wooden crate to a dusty pickup truck. His muscles bulged out of his rolled-up sleeves. He reminded me of Tarzan a little, except for the gray hair. He reminded me of my dad, too. Except for all the muscles.

The man saw me. "Good morning, young lady," he said. "You new here?" And he smiled.

My face flamed up. He couldn't tell what I was thinking, could he? I nodded and walked off, keeping my head up and my back straight. I didn't let myself look back at him.

I passed some side streets with houses, and I pictured those rich kids with the bikes living in the nicest one. A little farther on the paved road was a rusty street sign: MAIN STREET. A few old trucks were parked by a filling station. I could see a few dim shapes of people inside a bar.

The front of a small wooden building said BANK, LOANS AVAILABLE, but the door was nailed shut. A red-white-and-blue barber pole stood in front of a barbershop, but the window was boarded up. After that was a row of more boarded-up store windows. There was no drugstore or dry-goods store. No five-and-ten. No movie house.

I wrinkled my nose. Something smelled sour, rotten. The smell led me around the corner and along the railroad tracks toward a tall brick building.

Next to the tracks, on a wooden platform, was a bench with VALLEY JUNCTION painted on it. The sign on the crummy building said VALLEY VISTA CANNERY. Beneath that, in smaller letters, it said Missouri's Finest.

A line of silent people wearing patched-up housedresses and overalls stood outside. Their faces were pinched and sad. They looked like the people standing in bread lines in the city. I knew what these people were waiting for. They were waiting, and hoping, for what must be the smelliest, worst job in the world.

I turned away fast and just then a delicate yellow butterfly fluttered by my face. I followed it around the corner and back down Main Street. I kept up with it, past the side streets with their few nice houses, past the grocery store with its Santa Claus and Tarzan flying through the air. I ran after it, past my ugly house across the tracks.

The butterfly sailed onto the bumpy dirt road. It zigzagged by old houses and barns; by scrawny chickens scratching in someone's dirt yard, and then—inside a fence—it flew by a bunch of real live black-and-white cows. I stopped and dug into my pocket. The paper and pencil were gone. All I could feel was a hole.

The cows lifted their heads from the grass and looked at me. I grabbed a stick and drew square cow shapes in the dirt.

Out of nowhere a car came barreling toward me, and I had to dive into a ditch by the road. The driver glared at me, and the dog inside barked. Stupid driver! I wasn't in his way.

I caught up with the butterfly just as it skimmed over a rickety fence. My mouth fell open. The wild yard was filled with butterflies; dozens of them, flitting like bits of gold over crayon-bright yellow and purple flowers.

I leaned against the gate. *"Watch out. . . . Be careful. . . . Never go into strange places. . . ."* And another time, *"Nice people don't barge in. . . ."* I shook my head to get rid of my mother's voice and pushed hard. The gate fell open, and I almost fell into the weeds. Something brushed against my leg, and I yelped. A furry gray thing made a path away from me through the grass.

I let out my breath. Only a cat. I was used to cats; there were plenty of strays in the city.

I held out my hand. "Here, kitty, here . . ."

And then I saw her.

She was in a chair under a dead-looking tree. Her old head, with its wrinkly face and wispy-white hair, was turned toward me. Was she smiling at me? And was that a toy, a *teddy* bear, on her lap?

"Hey, Charley!"

I whirled around. The two kids were on the road.

I ran out through the gate.

Mikey squeaked, "What the heck were you doing in crazy Beryl Stubbs' place?"

They must have finished their pancakes already, probably slopped with butter and syrup. "I don't know," I said. "I think it was the . . ."

"Wanna know what we did last summer?" He poked me. "We snuck in and stole Beryl Stubbs' watermelons, right from under her nose. And know what she did? While we were busy swiping them she asked us in for tea! We just grabbed the melons and ran! Mom said you can never tell what a crazy old lady will do, especially one who has a hobo for a boyfriend." Mikey's mouth turned down into a pout. "She made us promise never to go in there again."

Maxine yanked him. "Let's go!"

He twisted away. "Once we even spied Beryl Stubbs and her boyfriend dancing around her yard and singing! When d'ya think he'll be back, Maxine?"

Maxine didn't bother to answer. "This is going to be the most boring summer of my whole life!" she groaned, looking sideways at me. "Nobody wants to live in Valley

Junction anymore, and my friends from Amesville are gone, too. Plus, Dad said we could only go to our summer cottage for three weeks! On top of all that, I have to babysit a bratty eight-year-old brother!" She tossed her curls. "C'mon, brat, let's get going to the river."

There was a river?

Before I could ask her about it, Maxine said, "See you sometime," and took off.

"Wait for me!" Mikey yelled, and pedaled after her.

"Every red-blooded nine-year-old American kid needs a bike," Daddy says.

I picture a beautiful blue one.

He lights a cigarette. "And I promise you'll get one soon."

I imagine it with a basket, and red, white, and blue streamers flying off the handlebars.

"But it'll have to wait till I get another job." Daddy looks at his watch, tells me to turn on the radio, then lies back on the sofa, blowing smoke rings. The galloping music comes on. I run to get a pencil and paper.

"Nowhere in the pages of history," the announcer is saying, "can one find a greater champion of justice. Return with us now to those thrilling days of yesteryear. The Lone Ranger rides again!"

Halfway through the program I'm finishing a drawing of Daddy as the Lone Ranger and me as his faithful companion, Tonto, when Mom drags herself through the door with a bag of groceries, breathing hard from all the stairs.

She dumps the bag on the card table, then stands, glaring

down at Daddy. "Why in hell are you home? I told them at the factory that you'd show up to sweep the place."

"Just wait till the end of this, Loretta."

"You said you'd go this time."

Daddy stubs out his cigarette. "I SAID just a minute, Loretta. We're about to have a shoot-out with the Butch Cavendish gang."

I sit, looking down at my drawing. I know one of her screaming fits is coming.

"I believed you when you said you'd take care of me. When you swore that you'd work hard, that we'd put some savings away so I could have some nice things, so that someday we'd have a home of our own. Instead I'm still trapped—still slaving to keep us one step ahead of the rent collector!"

"Hold it, Loretta. Stop your ranting. You know I can't take just any job."

"Why did you say you'd go if you thought it was beneath you? It makes me look like a fool!"

I look back and forth between Mom and Daddy. He's right, of course. Daddy can't take any old job. He should be making movies, should be . . .

Then she yells at me. "You think your dad is such a hero? If it were up to him we'd be starving, living on the street. Ask him! He couldn't even hold that job selling candy on the railroad cars. He should be living on a train. In a boxcar with the other bums!"

Daddy's face turns white, then red, and his hands make fists. He gets up. He moves like a man made of wood.

"Daddy!"

He doesn't seem to hear me. He goes to the cabinet and opens its door. He begins to shovel out the pink-and-white dishes Mom is buying on the installment plan.

Mom rushes at him, but he holds her off.

On the radio, shots ring out. The Lone Ranger says, "I hope we're not too late, Tonto."

And then Daddy throws them. Two dishes. Three dishes.

Mom is screaming.

Four dishes!

She claws and pounds at him.

Crashing! Crashing! All of the dishes crashing against the wall.

I sit frozen. The splinters shiver on the floor.

"You all right, kemo sabe?"

"Yes, Tonto, the homesteaders are safe. We can leave now."

Mom sinks down on the floor. She covers her face with her hands.

Then the galloping music. A fiery horse with the speed of light, a cloud of dust, a hearty "Hi-yo, Silver . . . Away!"

And Daddy goes into the bedroom, packs his suitcase, and walks out the door.

I saw that Maxine and Mikey had disappeared over a hill.

I wiped my face dry of my babyish tears and trudged up the road behind them. Even if they didn't invite me, they can't keep me from seeing a river.

3
The Hiding-Place Tree

There were a few more run-down houses on the dirt road, a few more scratching chickens. A green grasshopper sprang out of the weeds, and a ladybug crawled up a stem. I'd only seen such creatures in schoolbooks before. In a field I saw a flash of bright blue—maybe a bluebird!

The sun was getting hotter; my stomach was feeling emptier. In a weedy field, some out-of-work people sat outside their flimsy shacks. I looked the other way, keeping my eyes peeled for more insects and birds.

Then I saw a place filled with crosses and gravestones, and with trees around the edges. The rusted iron gate was open.

Most of the gravestones tilted crazily. Others had fallen completely over and were covered with moss. The writing on some of the gravestones was so worn I couldn't read the names. I parted the weeds growing

over the tallest one. In carved letters it told the world
IN MEMORY OF OUR BELOVED HUSBAND AND FATHER.

Where was my dad now? Was he watching another
Tarzan movie this very minute? Laughing over Mickey
Mouse or Laurel and Hardy? Making a movie of his
own? I hugged myself to cover the ache, went out of the
graveyard, and started up the hill.

From the top of the hill I looked down on bursts of
sunlight sparkling on water. I walked slowly down, my
eyes glued on the shimmery river.

The kids' bikes were sprawled on the right side of the
road, just before a wooden bridge, and when I got close
I sneaked behind a tree to spy on them. Something small
jumped on the shore—a frog—and Mikey yelled and tried
to grab it.

I backed away and darted across the road. A path
wound alongside the river and I kept walking till I
couldn't hear the kids' voices.

The shore was full of smooth pebbles, all of them pret-
tier than any I'd collected from empty lots in the city,
and a tree with long, drooping branches hung over the
water. I slipped under the branches and was instantly in
a soft, green house, hidden from everyone.

The long leaves rustled like somebody sighing. A bird
called from somewhere, and another bird answered. My
stomach complained, wanting the peanut butter I'd left
at home. I watched the river change from green, to
brown, to the colors of the sky.

Close to shore the water was quiet, but in the middle

of the river leaves and twigs swept swiftly by. The twigs looked helpless, there was no way they could stop, no way they could go back—no way they could change what was happening to them.

I scrambled out from under the tree, picked up a stone, and threw it as hard as I could. It missed the twigs, splashed and disappeared. I threw another. I threw another. I threw stones till my arm was numb.

I stooped over the bank and stared down into the water. Like a shadowy ghost, my face stared back at me. Around my head was a halo of white clouds, and behind that, a reflection of the sky.

The longer I stared, the deeper the sky seemed to go; it looked as if it went on forever. If I leaned over more I could fall right through it, slowly, gently . . .

I felt dizzy and drew back. I was afraid of water. I couldn't swim.

4
Beryl Stubbs

The whistle shrieked; the wheels rumbled; the whole house shook. The screen door banged shut after my mother.

Downstairs, I couldn't find the milk, then I remembered. There was no Frigidaire anymore. No radio, either. No sofa, no buffet. Our last landlady, Mrs. Krenkel, had made sure of that. There were no pink-and-white dishes.

In a packing box I found a bowl, a spoon, and an open box of cornflakes. I poured out the cereal, mixed in tap water, and plunked myself down at the card table. I read the note on the table:

> Charlotte, it looks like I'll have to work overtime almost every day, even weekends, for the whole summer.
> So I won't be home until after dark. Take care

of yourself, don't stray too far, and go to bed early.

I'll look in on you when I get home.

Mother

I gulped down the cereal.

The clock kept ticking. Ticking.

I ran out of the house, crossed over the railroad tracks, and headed up the bumpy dirt road.

Inside the old lady's fence, so many butterflies were dipping and diving and chasing each other I couldn't even begin to count them. She was there again, in the chair under the tree. She was still holding the teddy bear. But this time her head was on her chest; she was asleep.

Behind the scraggly tree was a house I hadn't noticed before. It looked as if it might have been white once. And by the porch steps, as if it was waiting for me, as if I could just go in and help myself to it, was a bike.

Slowly, carefully, I pushed open the gate. It only groaned a little. The gray cat came through the weeds, rubbed against me, and purred. The grass swished.

"Are you here for tea?"

I froze.

Beryl Stubbs' face was crisscrossed with lines. Her eyes were blue pinpoints, half hidden in baggy pouches of skin.

"We're having graham crackers today. We love graham crackers. Do you?"

My mouth watered.

"I'm Mrs. Leon Stubbs," she went on, as if I'd answered her. "What's your name?"

Her voice was young, not old at all.

A butterfly danced in the air between us. "What is your name, child?" she asked again.

The way she said *child* made me feel funny, made my insides hurt. Or was it just my stomach wanting the graham crackers.

"Charley," I answered.

I waited for her to say it was a boy's name, to ask who I was, what I was doing in her yard. But all she said was, "I am glad to meet you, Charley." The wrinkles around her mouth turned up, and she stuck out her hand. "I'd like you to call me by my first name, too. People around here call me Beryl."

What they *really* call you is crazy, I thought.

Beryl Stubbs kept smiling. Her outstretched hand was crooked and covered with brown spots and lumpy blue veins.

Her hand stayed in the air; I had to take it. I was surprised—it felt warm and dry, and had a strong grip on mine.

"And this," she pointed to the cat at her feet, "is Sweet Pea. Named after Popeye's baby boy. I like Popeye. Don't you?"

I had to nod. I did like Popeye.

The old lady finally let go of my hand. "I knew you did," she said. "I can tell about people."

I didn't tell her Popeye's baby's name was really

Swee' Pea. Talking about cartoon characters with an old person was *crazy*.

Clutching the teddy bear, which had hardly any fur and no eyes, Beryl Stubbs pushed down on the arms of the chair. I stood on one foot, then another as she hoisted herself up and reached for a cane. Finally she took a wobbly breath and said, "It's time for our tea."

Her back was stooped; she was even shorter than me. Her shoes were crunched down in the back like slippers, and her faded, flowery dress hung on her like a sack and made me conscious of my own secondhand clothes.

"The only thing is . . . " She frowned. "We can't have you holding Tommy's teddy bear just yet. He still doesn't like to share his toys. That is, until he knows you better."

I looked around. Who was she talking about? Nobody else was there.

"But," she made a move toward me and I backed away. "I'm sure Tommy likes you. He has a way of knowing about people, too." She smiled. "We're both glad to have company again."

I took another step back. She reminded me of the bent-over witch who invited Hansel and Gretel into her house and made them captives. Well, I could run faster than an old lady, could get away easy if I had to.

But then Beryl Stubbs did something. And I got that tight feeling in my middle again. She put her hand on the tree and patted it. That was what I used to do. When I was little, I'd pretend that any tree I could find was my friend.

Sweet Pea sprang to the house ahead of us. I followed after the old lady, but kept a safe distance between us.

The cat waited on the slanty porch steps. Brambly vines grew up the side of the house and hung down over the roof. A broken porch swing lay in one corner and two rocking chairs and a table sat like three old people by the torn screen door.

The bike leaning against the steps was rusty. Its tires were flat.

Beryl Stubbs put her cane on the first step, then one foot, then the other, before going up to the next. At the screen door, she turned. "Make yourself at home, child. I'll be out in a jiffy with the tea."

I put my hands on the bike. The handlebars wouldn't turn. Over a fence by the side of the house, some black-and-white cows were watching me.

I gave up on the bike and climbed onto the top rung of the fence.

Yellow butterflies chased each other into the field. The cows put down their heads and munched on purple flowers, and there was a kind of humming in the air. And everything smelled different. There was no stink of garbage or of trucks, and none of the other city smells, either. I took a breath. What was it? It smelled clean, but more than that. I took another breath. It smelled green.

Suddenly one cow gave a loud *moo* and started walking toward me. I slid off that fence so fast I nearly fell backward. I looked around. Only the cat had seen me.

Beryl Stubbs came out with a tray. Sweet Pea leaped

on the table, and the old lady gave him milk in a saucer. She motioned me to a rocking chair and held out a plate. I took a graham cracker; it was crispy-good. She offered me more, and I stuffed two in my mouth. I drank three cups of tea with milk and sugar. The only sounds were the cat lapping and me drinking. I tried not to slurp.

Now she'd ask me: Who was I? Who were my parents? What did they do? But the old lady just sipped her tea and rocked back and forth, the vines making patterns of leafy sun and shade on her face. A robin flew down below the steps. Sweet Pea saw the bird, too, and I grabbed him before he could pounce. The robin flew away, but I kept my arms around the cat's soft, furry body.

Beryl Stubbs kept rocking. I rocked a little, too.

I noticed a small, dark shape on the vine. It looked different from the leaves, moved differently, too. It shook, like something was pushing from the inside. All at once a tiny head poked through. I jumped up. Sweet Pea meowed and dropped off my lap. It was a butterfly! A butterfly was coming out of a cocoon.

The butterfly pulled and stretched. I stood as close as I dared.

It wiggled and stretched and pulled—and stopped.

I hardly breathed.

It stretched again—struggled, pulled—trying to get loose.

At last—slowly, slowly—the butterfly wiggled free.

Suddenly I heard, "There's Charley!"

I spun around. It was Mikey, on his bike, with Maxine right behind him.

"See her, Maxine?" Mikey yelled. "Charley's on crazy Beryl Stubbs's porch!"

My cheeks burned. The kids rode past.

I looked sideways at the old lady.

Her eyes were closed. She began to hum.

The teddy bear she was hugging was blind, but it seemed to be staring at me. It felt like the hole in the screen door was looking at me, too. Even the broken porch swing, the old tree in the yard, the rusty bike . . . .

The butterfly's wings were squished and wet. It was so weak it could hardly hold on to the empty cocoon.

And I recognized the tune the old lady was humming.

I ran down the porch steps and out the gate.

It was a baby song. *Twinkle, Twinkle, Little Star.*

> Twinkle, twinkle little star,
> How I wonder what you are.
> Up above the world so high . . .

Dolly's painted blue eyes gaze so trustfully up at me. I hold her close as I sing.

"Look what I've made for your baby, Charlotte." Mama shows me a tiny blue pillow circled with ruffles. She's already sewn Dolly a nightgown to match the blue dress she'd made for me.

I lay Dolly in her shoe-box cradle and carefully place the new pillow under her head. Then I get out my crayons and make a picture of Dolly, Mama, Daddy, and me. I use every one of my seven colors to draw the sky and the grass, and the flowers and birds all around us.

"Mama," I say, "let's get us a real baby, a new baby sister or brother."

Mama takes a quick look at my picture. "Babies cost money," she says, like she always does. I see up and down lines worry between her eyes.

"Charlotte, I have something to tell you. Your daddy is out of work. We'll have to move again."

"Poor Daddy! Is he sad? Will he get another job? How will we buy food?"

Mama looks away. "Of course he'll find another job," she says. "But for now I'll have to work more hours at the dress factory."

My chest feels tight. "I don't want you to!"

"Just think, Charlotte. If we earn more money, we won't have to move so much. And someday we'll have a home of our own, with everything nice that you can imagine."

Mama likes nice things. She has lots of magazines that show pictures of pretty ladies and dishes and houses.

"I don't care," I yell. "I don't want you to work more!"

"You're six years old now, Charlotte, a big girl. You'll be staying with Mrs. Smith downstairs. I know you'll be brave while I'm gone. That you'll behave nicely, too."

I wrap my arms tight around her.

"You will be brave, won't you?"

I swallow.

I look up into Mama's sad blue eyes and nod.

5
The Mannings

I straggled up the dirt road. I straggled down. I scuffed up the dust with my sneakers. I crossed over the tracks and stopped at home for spoonfuls of peanut butter, then went out again.

I came back, sat in the kitchen, went up to my room. The attic was boiling hot. I took my scrap paper and pencils down to the card table.

One of my scribbled shapes looked like a cocoon. I drew a butterfly's head coming out. I made another picture—of the butterfly flying away.

But it *hadn't* flown away. I'd run off while its wings were still crumpled. Now I'd never know if the butterfly ever got its wings to work, would never know if it even got to live.

I scrunched up my drawings, went out the door, and

wandered up and down the road again. I stayed away from the town, stayed away from the cannery.

One minute I told myself I only wanted to see where they lived. The next minute I knew I wanted to tell Maxine about the butterfly, that I saw a butterfly being born. But should I tell her? And about the bike? Especially about the bike—that I sneaked in to steal it? They thought they were so brave sneaking in to steal the old lady's watermelons. Stealing a bike was much more daring. And they had run away when Beryl Stubbs invited them to tea. I'd had the nerve to stay.

I could see Maxine and me slinking into Beryl Stubbs' yard at night, me leading the way, snooping around—even seeing what she had in her house. Maxine would be sorry about turning her back and riding away. Why, she'd even let me borrow her bike. But—my mind kept spinning—I'd have to find somewhere private where I could learn how to ride.

The sun was almost down by the time I put my nose against the grocery's screen door. Inside someone announced, "Here comes the pitch."

I waited. The radio voice yelled, "It's a hit!"

I put my hand on the doorknob.

"He's safe! It's a home run! The game is over! St. Louis wins three to two!" There was a big roar from the radio and clapping from inside the store.

I straightened my shoulders and pulled open the door.

From force of habit, my eyes darted to the shelves.

There were cans of food; boxes of crackers; bread and candy bars; and a jar of jelly beans. On the floor sat barrels labeled "Flour," "Rice," "Beans," and a keg of nails. There were no crayons or paints. No pencils. A used pencil lay on the counter.

"Well, hello again." The grocery-store man turned off the radio.

"Uh," I cleared my throat. "Is there any mail for me?"

"You're the Gordon girl, right? Moved into the old brick house by the tracks? Nope, no mail so far."

I stood.

He waited.

"Can you tell me where Maxine Manning lives?" My voice came out too loud.

"The Mannings?" His face changed. "You really want to know?"

My head down, I nodded.

"OK. Well, the Mannings live on the only street with a sidewalk." He came to the door and pointed. "It's down the road that way. First side street. Big, white house, green shutters."

I could feel him watching as I started off in that direction.

Maxine's and Mikey's bikes lay inside a white picket fence. The grass was clipped short, and there wasn't one weed, not even a dandelion. Through the window I saw a pretty blond-haired lady setting out dishes on a white tablecloth. It was like a picture–like the cover of one of my mother's magazines. Even outside I could smell something delicious. Maybe what I liked best—thick vegetable soup.

I could baby-sit Mikey, clean the house. Mrs. Manning might even ask me to move in with them.

I shuffled up the block. I shuffled back. I kicked a pebble, then kicked it back. I'd be good with the boy. I'd do whatever needed to be done. And Maxine must have whole boxes of crayons and paints and paper. But, of course, the mother would pay me. I'd find out where I could buy my own paints—I'd buy a bike. . . .

A car came up the street, and I crouched down by the fence in front of the Mannings' house. The car stopped, and a big man with wide shoulders stepped out and walked through the gate. The football-star father.

Before Mr. Manning reached the door, it opened. Soft lights glowed from inside, and Maxine ran out and said, "Hi, Daddy. Your supper's ready."

I took a breath and stood up.

Maxine saw me and stared past her dad.

He turned around, looked me up and down, and said, "Well, well, what have we here?"

With one hand I tried to cover a tear in my shorts. He laughed.

The mother stepped outside. "What's going on?"

I opened my mouth. Nothing came out.

All three of them stood on the steps by the open door. Then Mikey squeezed in between his folks and announced, "It's Charley! Hey, Charley, what're you doing here?"

Mrs. Manning looked down at me.

"Sorry, dear," she said, "we don't give handouts at this house."

Then everyone moved.

The dad marched inside, saying, "Let's eat!"

Maxine followed him.

The mother hustled Mikey in.

With a click, the door closed behind her.

My mother closes the door of our basement apartment. I stand with her on the stoop. Down the block, a stranger is carting away our almost-paid-for Frigidaire.

Through the first-floor window I see our landlady, Mrs. Krenkel, putting her dishes into our cabinet. Her husband is turning the knobs on our radio. Our overstuffed, maroon sofa is against their wall. All of them were payment for overdue rent. They would have taken our nice dishes, too. If we still had them.

Everything we still own is piled in the pickup truck parked on the street—our suitcases of clothes; my mother's matching bed and dresser set; my cot; the card table and chairs; cardboard boxes with food and kitchen stuff; my mother's magazines; and my art box. She'd made me leave behind my collection of empty lot pebbles, but I was able to slip by her with my paper and pencil stubs.

My mother looks at me. Her peroxide-blond hair isn't neatly curled the way it used to be. Her fingernail polish is chipped and doesn't match her lipstick. "It's what you wanted, isn't it?" Her voice sounds flat. "Moving to the country. Like your everlasting drawings of trees and flowers, birds and bees. Well, maybe it will be better. Nicer people. Away from bad influences."

Away from HIM, *she means, in case he comes back.*

Mrs. Krenkel comes outside, her long face stern as always. "So you're off," she says to my mother. "I have to hand it to you, Loretta. You lose one job, and even if it's in some out-of-the-way, godforsaken place, you find another." She folds her big arms across her chest. "That's one thing about you, Loretta. You do keep on."

My mother turns to go. "Yes."

For the third time, I tell Mrs. Krenkel our new address: General Delivery, Valley Junction, Missouri. "In case my dad . . ."

Mrs. Krenkel nods.

I don't move.

"Stop daydreaming, Charlotte. I've hired this driver and his truck for today, not tomorrow."

Squeezed into the front seat, I hold myself away from my mother and her perfume. Mrs. Krenkel lifts one hand in a short wave good-bye. The streetlights flicker and turn on. The truck pulls away.

"So you're off to live in the wide open spaces," the truck driver says.

I sneak a look. My mother's mouth is a straight line.

"Making a fresh start, eh?"

No answer.

"You're the lucky one, finding a job these days."

"Yes. And I'm paying you my last dollar. We'd better get there tonight."

"Don't worry, lady."

We rattle through the streets, the buildings getting smaller, the telephone poles farther apart, the sky darker. I press my face against the truck window and watch the moon traveling along with us.

The next thing I know, the truck is bumping over railroad tracks.

"This is it?" My mother's voice sounds screechy.

"It's the address you gave me, lady. Looks like you're living in the middle of nowhere."

6
The Garden

Outside, the morning train rumbled. Downstairs, the door banged shut. And I was still raging about yesterday at Maxine's. I reached under my cot, dragged out my paper and pencil stubs, and made a mess of lines turn into Maxine covered with horrible bumps and hair like wriggling snakes. Another scribble turned into her mother—a rat with a long rat tail. Still another became her father, with a devil's horns, a pig's nose, and fangs.

I stamped downstairs. There was a note on a bit of torn envelope.

> There are cans of chicken noodle soup in a
> box. I'm late. Take care of yourself.

Something silver shone on the table. A quarter.

A quarter could buy me five candy bars, or five double-dipped ice cream cones. I squeezed the money in my fist. It could buy me pencils—if there were any to buy. I ran up to my room and threw the quarter into my suitcase. I might need the money later. I might run away.

I left the house. Stalking up the dirt road—kicking at the dust and any stones in my way—I squinched my face into a horrible smile, picturing all four *Ms* with hideous Halloween skull faces. I was so busy making them into more and more gruesome monsters that I almost bumped into the grocery store truck. Beryl Stubbs and the grocery man were standing by her gate.

"I am happy to see you, Charley," the old lady said.

Had she forgotten about yesterday? That I'd run off while she was still singing the baby song? That I hadn't even said good-bye?

"Come and meet Don," she was saying.

The grocery man pumped my hand up and down. "Glad to know you, Charley. We've met a couple of times already, right? I'm glad to welcome you to our hole-in-the-wall town. Of course, except for the cannery and the train stop, you've probably discovered there's not much of anything in Valley Junction these days. But it's not as bad as it looks. In a few months you'll be bused to school in Amesville, twenty miles out past the cannery. Then you'll have it better."

My face burned. From the way he was going on, he probably guessed what had happened at the Mannings'.

He finally let go of my hand.

I hated that I always got red, hated that I felt it all the way from the bottom of my neck to the top of my head.

"But I'm glad you've discovered my friend Beryl."

I kept my eyes on my sneakers.

"I'll bring your milk and eggs later, Beryl. More ice for your icebox, too. And Charley," Don held open the gate, "I hope to see you here again."

I watched his truck bounce away over the ruts in the road.

"Poor Don," Beryl Stubbs was mumbling, "his wife gone, and now his children grown and gone, too." She turned and looked at me. "Not so long ago, you know, Don and Tommy were playing together."

Tommy again. Who was Tommy, anyway? It was graham crackers I wanted to hear about.

On the porch, one rocking chair held the teddy bear. A ratty baby doll was in the other. The old lady motioned me to the chair with the doll, then limped into the house. I picked up the doll, didn't know what to do with it, so I held it and sat down. Sweet Pea jumped onto my lap, and I held him, too.

Beryl Stubbs came out with the tea tray. Just as she eased herself into her rocker, a yellow butterfly sailed onto the porch. "Here he is!" The old lady laughed and clapped her hands. "Here's the butterfly you saw being born."

I hoped she was right. But how did she know it was the same one? And how did she know it was a boy?

The butterfly opened and closed its wings. The old lady hugged the teddy bear. "Our butterfly is having a fine time in the world," she said. "Can't you just tell?"

Crazy. I held onto Sweet Pea and gobbled graham crackers.

We rocked. Both of our chairs creaked. The butterfly fluttered off.

The old lady stopped rocking and peered at me. "Your folks both work?"

I gave a short nod and looked away.

She sipped her tea, and I squirmed. Even somebody crazy knew I didn't have any other place to go.

All at once, she put down her cup, and held onto her side. After a minute she said, "I could use some help."

For money?

Beryl Stubbs reached into her apron pocket, but all she brought out were some small envelopes covered with pictures of bright-colored vegetables. The colors looked good enough to eat.

"It's late for planting," she said. "And, to tell you the truth, I didn't know if I could this year, didn't know if I had the gumption." She smiled at me. "But all that's changed now–now that you've come to me."

Huh? I knew I should be getting out of there. But I just sat and waited. I wanted to know about the envelopes in her hands.

"Another thing," the old lady's face turned into worry lines, "the seeds in these packets are from two years ago. I'm not sure . . ." Her hands trembled as she touched the picture of the watermelon. "But Tommy does love water-melon, you know."

The mysterious Tommy. I gritted my teeth, thinking of

those thieving Mannings. *They* loved her watermelons, too.

"So we are going to plant a garden, Charley." Beryl Stubbs put the seed packets back in her pocket and pushed down on the arms of her chair. "We are going to plant it now!"

She started down the steps without her cane, stumbled, and lost her balance. I jumped up and grabbed her before she fell headfirst. Just as quick, I let go of her at the bottom.

When she got between the porch and the dead tree, she slipped off her shoes and stepped onto a patch of prickly-looking straw. I gawked at her knobby, leathery-hard feet. They looked like they could walk on anything.

She picked up a bit of straw with her toes. "And this straw keeps it warm all winter. Keeps the seeds safe, too, while they're sprouting."

Little by little she let herself down on the straw. She dug into her pocket again and handed me a big spoon. "Get down here with me," she ordered, "and make the holes just deep enough so the seeds can spread out their roots."

I was sure the old lady couldn't pay me. So why was I crawling on my hands and knees, taking her orders, digging holes through her straw, and getting all hot and dirty? I glanced at her squeezing the dirt through her fingers and crumbling it, holding it to her nose, and taking deep, smiling breaths.

I took a tiny sniff. The dirt had a strange new smell,

strong and damp. I sniffed at the straw—it smelled hot and dry. I had to admit it. They both smelled exactly how I'd imagined it would smell out in the country.

Then Beryl Stubbs gave me some of the vegetable seeds to put in the holes. She crawled on her knees, sticking seeds into holes, too. "Easier on all fours," she told me. Even so, she was breathing hard, her wrinkles hanging down and her face sweaty.

After we planted she had me cover the seeds with more dirt and straw and pat it all down. And *then* she asked me to go to her spigot, get the hose, and water the whole thing.

"It will be your job to keep our garden happy this summer, Charley." Her old face was beaming.

I wondered if I should get away now. OK, so I did like the smells here. I liked the graham crackers. I liked the butterflies. But *happy? Our* garden?

All at once something poked out of the straw. I gasped and jumped back.

"That's Walt," the old lady said.

Walt?

The ugly little dinosaur thing had scaly skin, a long, scaly tail, and claws for feet.

"Always has been a lizard or two around here."

The thing scurried off to a patch of sun.

Beryl Stubbs chuckled. "And they're all named Walt."

7
Her House

A giant lizard, turning this way and that, roaming through the darkness. A tiny, golden butterfly landing between his blind eyes and going inside his head. It was the strangest dream. At least it wasn't like most of my dreams—me stuck in a hole, or lost; me running from one house to another, never the right one. I was about to reach under my cot for a pencil and paper when I felt a cool hand on my arm.

"Wake up, Charlotte."

I didn't move.

"Charlotte, I have a little time. Come downstairs with me."

I opened my eyes a slit. My mother's light blue house-dress matched her eyes; her lipstick was bright red. She was slipping bobby pins into her bleached-blond hair. I tried to hold on to the butterfly and the lizard in my head.

In the kitchen, she poured out her coffee and sat down

at the card table. Her used lady's magazine lay open to a picture of a blond woman standing by a polished wood dining-room set.

"Now, tell me," she said, "what have you been doing with yourself?"

I shook cornflakes into a bowl, added water, sat down, and picked up my spoon. I couldn't tell if she was looking at the woman or the dining-room set.

"Well?"

"Oh." The cereal floated in the water. "I'm helping somebody with her garden."

"That's nice."

Her eyes flickered over me, then away. "Is her mother home?"

"Yes," I lied.

"Is she a nice girl?"

I pictured Beryl's wrinkled face and almost laughed.

"Well, *is* she?"

"Yes," I said, "she's *nice.*"

"What's her name?"

"Uh–Maxine." She would *love* blond-and-pink Maxine.

"What's her last name?"

"Manning."

My mother's head snapped up. "Did you say Manning?"

"That's right."

"You met Mrs. Manning?"

I nodded.

"What's she like?"

"She's–she's nice."

The morning train screeched past, and my mother's coffee cup shook along with the house. "I know about Mrs. Manning," she said. "I wish I had *her* life."

I kept my head down.

She stood, reached for her cracked, red-leather purse, took out a quarter, and said, "I have to go, can't be late."

I looked up. She seemed worn out already.

"But I'm glad," she said. "I'm very glad you've made friends with the Manning girl. They're the right kind of people, the kind of people I never had the chance to know."

I stared at the cornflakes, sunk into a soggy mess.

"Another thing, Charlotte." At the kitchen door she was all business again. "Please iron your clothes and comb your hair. And don't ever chop off your hair again the way you did. People judge you by how you look. You need to make a good impression."

The screen door banged behind her.

I went into the bathroom and ripped my mother's peroxide strands out of the hairbrush. In the mirror, I stared at my plain face and my sticking-out hair.

I need to make a good impression?

I knew where she kept the scissors.

But all I ended up doing was slamming the kitchen door.

Wading through the weeds, I saw a butterfly flit around Beryl Stubbs under the bare tree, and I thought of the golden butterfly in my dream. At the edge of the garden I looked for Walt, the lizard, not sure what I'd do if he suddenly popped up.

I spotted him sunning on the porch railing, so I pulled off my shoes and stepped onto the straw. The garden looked exactly like it did before, a bunch of straw spread out. I doubted that anything would come up.

"I was just now talking to Tommy," the old lady was saying.

Tommy *again!* The straw pricked my feet, and I winced. "Who's Tommy?" I asked.

She gazed at me, a bewildered look on her face, then shook her head. "I get mixed up, child. I thought for a minute that you and Tommy were friends." She patted the tree. "Tommy's my boy. I planted this apple tree the spring he was born. I've been telling him about you."

"About *me?*"

"Of course, child. I tell my boy all that's in my heart–the garden and the butterflies–and the good, sweet people."

Me? Good? And *sweet?*

Another lizard poked out of the straw. I jumped back, and he and I stared at each other. I had a feeling he'd made his own judgment about me, and that it didn't agree with Beryl's.

"You been to the river?" The old lady was still talking. I nodded.

The puzzled look came into her eyes again. She shook her head, struggled to her feet, and said, "It's time for tea."

Good. I was ready.

She moved even more slowly than before. On the porch, she sank into a rocking chair. I volunteered to make the tea.

In the kitchen, I looked in the icebox. There was only a little milk and butter. In the cupboard I found just tea and sugar, some bread, and half a box of graham crackers. Beryl Stubbs was like Old Mother Hubbard in the nursery rhyme, who was so poor she couldn't give her dog a bone. She was even poorer than us. I stuffed two crackers in my mouth.

I peeked out the screen door. Her head was on her chest; she was asleep. I was alone in the old lady's house.

Everything in her front room was worn out: the potbellied stove in the corner, the yellowed doilies and the lumpy sofa, the dried-up flowers in jelly jars. Gray cobwebs hung from the ceiling, and old toys and stuffed animals were piled everywhere.

I picked up a rusty toy truck. So she really must have a boy named Tommy, like she said—her boy she planted the apple tree for. But the tree was old now, its branches were bare. Beryl Stubbs was old. Wouldn't Tommy be all grown up now, even old himself? He must have moved away somewhere, probably to escape from her. People did escape from their mothers, didn't they? My hands made fists. They escaped from their wives, too.

Beryl Stubbs' walls were covered with old magazine pictures, all of them yellowed and curled up at the edges. The pictures were mostly of far-away animals; elephants and whales and giraffes, and of faraway places; oceans, deserts, jungles, and mountains. I stared at a snowy peak rising above a gold-clouded sky.

It would be a hard climb, but I could see myself escaping to that mountain, could see myself there at the very top. In the valley far below I could see my mother, then Maxine and Maxine's mother, all staring up at me in awe. But I wouldn't even look down at them. I'd be too busy up there, painting the world's most beautiful picture of a sunset.

I blinked, and the picture in my head was gone. I let myself feel a shiver of pleasure anyhow.

The house had three bedrooms. Two were stuffed with wicker chests, magazines, comic books, and more toys. The third had an old-fashioned oval mirror and a double bed, covered with a faded patchwork quilt. *Her* room. I could see the bare tree through the window. And the bunch of straw on the ground.

There was a chest of drawers.

I looked over my shoulder. Nobody.

I listened. No sound from the porch.

I opened the drawers. Just clothes and handkerchiefs and a few old letters. I picked up the lone fountain pen. I caught a glimpse of myself in the mirror. I put the pen down.

A worn photo album lay on the bed. Inside were old brown pictures, the people in long, dark clothes. On one page, a big man with squinty eyes and his arm around a happy-faced girl, was grinning. The girl's hair was dark, but I could still tell that she was Beryl Stubbs. It was the way she was looking out at me, and her smile. Under a photograph of a thin man with a mustache was written, "Leon." The last page showed a young Beryl Stubbs holding a laughing, dark-haired baby. The baby's eyes looked out at me, too.

Her rocker out on the porch creaked. I went back to the kitchen, found matches, and lit the stove to heat up water for tea.

At home later, I rummaged through the unpacked boxes. There had been a picture. I was a baby and my mother was holding me. My dad had taken the snapshot with his box camera. I knew I wouldn't find any pictures of *him*; she'd thrown them out long before.

I went up the stairs and lay on my cot. Did I remember enough to draw a picture of him? I remembered he was handsome. I remembered his blue suit and red tie, and his gray felt hat cocked over one eye, and the way his cigarette dangled from his mouth. I remembered the day he came walking down the street and me running to meet him, and him swinging me around and us dancing a few steps. But his face. I couldn't remember my dad's face.

The kitchen door opened.

I flopped over and pretended to be asleep.

8
The Cannery

The note said:

> I see we're out of cornflakes.
> Here is something else to eat.
> And I hope you like the clothes.
> Have a good time with your friend.
> —Mother

A can of peas stood on the card table. "Green 'n' Good from Valley Vista," the label said, with a picture of bright green peas in a row. Next to the can lay blue jeans, shorts, and a blouse.

I didn't like the tan-colored blouse, but at least it fit me—it didn't hang like a tent, or else squeeze me in. And the blue jeans had two big pockets, without holes. I found a safety pin to hold up the waist and rolled up the cuffs.

I found the can opener and managed to open the peas.

Spooning them up, I noticed the wrinkled paper bag on the table. Inside were four peanut-butter-and-soda-cracker sandwiches.

My mother's lunch.

I washed my spoon and her coffee cup. I emptied a cardboard box and arranged the cans of chicken noodle soup next to the jar of peanut butter in the cupboard. I wiped off the table. Then I opened the door to my mother's room.

Her old, pink chenille bathrobe lay in a tangle of sheets on her bed. A magazine was open to a picture of a shiny clean family: a mother, a father, and two dimpled children. The mother had long, red fingernails. More magazines were piled on the floor. Face powder was spilled on her dresser, together with a used-up bottle of perfume and a cake of mascara, almost cracked dry.

I checked her dresser drawers. There were a few lace handkerchiefs, some underwear. In the bottom drawer, face down, under her best blue blouse, I found pictures. A snapshot of her when she was a girl, looking skinny and mad. And the one I remembered, of me in her arms.

I held the picture. Was I ever so chubby and cute? Was she ever so beautiful and happy? We were both smiling at the camera. Smiling at my dad taking the picture.

My blue-jean pockets felt suddenly empty. I slipped the snapshots back in the drawer, ran up to my room, and stuffed the pockets with paper and pencil stubs.

Downstairs, I snatched up the bag with the crackers and went out the kitchen door.

Outside the cannery, the smell was still awful; the people looking for work still waited. I heard one man tell another, "Them peas out back stink worse than a hog pit." I pulled back my shoulders, marched through the line of people–they smelled bad, too–and went straight to the big door.

I turned the heavy doorknob. The door wouldn't open. I jiggled it and pushed it. I felt the sad eyes behind me. I knocked. Nothing.

"You have to knock harder, girlie," a scruffy man said.

I pounded with my fist.

The door opened a crack, and I blurted, "I have to see my mother."

"What for?"

"She forgot her food."

"Nobody's allowed in." The guard looked down at me. "OK, for a minute. But don't let the boss see you."

He pulled me inside. The door slammed in the scruffy man's face.

Tin cans clanged and clattered along an assembly line. Men shouted orders, other men pulled the cans into cooling tanks, and over it all was the gray grinding noise of machines. The guard pointed to the stairs. The noise followed me like a monster to the second floor.

The thick clouds of steam almost hid the rows of women, stooped over, sorting and washing big trays of peas. I walked up one row and down the other till I found her. I stood behind her for a minute, then touched her shoulder.

My mother swiveled around. Her face was shiny with sweat; her hair was frizzy. She snapped, "What are you doing here?" Black mascara dripped down her cheeks.

I gave her the bag. Her hand brushed mine. Her eyes slid over me, then away.

The woman next to her said, "So this is your kid, eh, Loretta? My daughter's clothes look good on her."

My mother pushed a can of peas at me. "Get out!" she hissed. "Do you want me to lose my job?"

A heavy, big-shouldered man strode out from between the rows of women. Maxine's dad! I ducked down.

My mother shoved me away from her. Hard.

I stood, blinking in the sun. I looked down at the can in my hand. My stomach ached. I walked stiffly away from the staring people.

And there were Maxine and Mikey, straddling their bikes, gawking at me. My legs felt shaky, but I managed to stick out my chin and stump past them.

I plodded down Main Street, past the men lolling by the gas station and the men on the curb with their bottles of beer, past the side streets, past the grocery store—past my house across the tracks.

My feet carried me up the dirt road.

I was at Beryl Stubbs' gate. I kept walking.

I heard their voices and jumped quick into the ditch. They rode by and I caught Mikey saying, "I didn't see her just now at crazy old Beryl's place. Where could she be? Maxine, d'ya think maybe *she's* crazy, too?"

Crouching in the ditch, my hands made fists. It wasn't hard to guess what Maxine had answered.

At the river I gathered up the prettiest stones I could find and threw them. Stone after stone after stone into the river. I pulled out a handful of paper, crumpled it up, and watched it swirl and sink. I wanted to throw the can of peas.

I sat under my tree.

I heard the sighing of the wind. I heard a bird call and another bird answer, heard the pebbly wash of the waves on the shore and the rippling sound in the middle of the river. I knew the colors of the river were changing, from green and brown to the colors of the sky. But I only saw my mother's eyes sliding away from me, my mother pushing me away.

The way she pushed *him*–the way she pushed him away for good.

And I sat.

My stomach growled fiercely. But I sat.

Sat until the sun hung in the trees. Sat until it shone a golden path on the water, sat until I couldn't sit anymore.

Then, the can tight in my hand, I trudged back.

To tea and graham crackers. To butterflies.

To Beryl.

9
Lucky

There she was. Still in her chair under the tree, still humming the baby song, still cradling the teddy bear. Still smiling at me coming in the gate. And, without warning, my anger rose up. Why did Beryl have to be so happy all the time? Didn't anything ever make her mad—or sad? Why did she always have to keep smiling? Why did she even want me around?

I marched up to her and dumped the can at her feet. Mothers, not crazy old ladies, were supposed to smile at you and want to be with you!

Beryl stooped and picked up the can.

I stomped over to the water spigot. Even though I was sure those old seeds wouldn't grow.

"Dented," Beryl said. "They sell the dented cans to the workers."

I turned my back.

"I had to work at that place once."

My eyes stung. I squeezed them shut.

"Come, child." That word again.

I stole a look. Beryl was holding out her arms to me.

I couldn't stop them—my hot tears spilled out.

"Charley, I want to tell you something. Something important. Something I never told anyone else."

I wiped my face with my fists, walked slowly over to Beryl, and sat down by her chair.

"It was the same time as now," she began, "the sun had just set and I was hurrying up the road, late getting supper. And I was thinking: What was the point of supper? What was the point of anything?" She stopped.

I raised my head.

"What I was feeling . . . what I was feeling . . . was that I could not go on."

I stared at her.

"Funny thing, though. Even so—even with the way I was feeling and all, I couldn't help but notice that the whole sky was flaming red, a brilliant red I'd never seen before. And then I saw the yellow butterfly. He was flying up the road in front of me. When he got up a ways he flew back. As if he knew me. As if he knew—what had happened."

Above us, a butterfly flitted through the branches. The low light circled around its wings and made it glow. I wanted to ask, "*What* happened?" But Beryl was going on.

"And that minute," she said, "everything changed."

I watched the butterfly float up and become a dark speck against the sky. "What do you mean *changed*?"

"That tiny sliver of life was telling me something. As plain as day, he said—" Beryl cupped her hands as if she were holding something out to me. "He told me, no matter how short a time we may be in this world, every one of us creatures—can you picture it?—every butterfly, every person, every . . ."

I waited. Beryl took a breath.

"—every child—every poor, beautiful one of us is here all together. Oh, Charley, I don't know how to say it." She spread out her arms. "The just plain wonder of it—to have life."

She leaned back. "Tell me. Wasn't I lucky I noticed that butterfly?"

The sky flamed. Everything was still. The light deepened the trees, the color of the weeds, the straw on the garden. Beryl's run-down house glowed red and orange and gold.

"And then," Beryl said, "I planted the weeds my caterpillars eat. And clover and alfalfa, because they give the flowers my butterflies like."

She reached down and touched my hair. "I've talked enough."

I looked at the ground. I looked up at the sky. I reached into my pocket for my pencil and last bit of paper. I smoothed out the paper and drew a butterfly coming out of a cocoon. I thought a minute, then made it waving one foot, and with a smile on its face.

"Charley!" Beryl clapped her hands. "That's just how it is! You're a real artist. You're double lucky."

I felt my mouth curve up like hers.

In bed, I tried to imagine a new family, a full table, an even fuller cupboard. But all I saw was old Beryl holding her arms out to me, telling me how lucky she was, how seeing the butterfly made everything change. A yellow butterfly flitted across my mind. Could things change for me?

The kitchen door groaned open, then my mother was on my stairs.

I turned over and lay still.

My mother stood by my door for a long time.

10
Bums and Dishes

The note on the kitchen table said:

> I'm getting off early today.
> Be home. I want to talk to you.

What about? Was she going to ask me about Maxine Manning? Or did she lose her job because I came to the cannery? The morning was already hot, but I felt a chill.

I got down on my knees and pushed the straw away from a hole. Something green was there. I uncovered more holes. Tiny plants were in every one. And every plant had two perfectly round little leaves.

"Beryl!" I shouted. "Things are growing!"

Beryl hobbled over. "Oh, yes." She laughed and patted my head. "I knew my babies would come up."

I filled up a watering can and dribbled water on every

green thing. And then, sitting on the porch, I covered the pages of Beryl's old telephone book with drawings of the new shapes in our garden.

Beryl took a sip of tea and said, "Your ma was here last night."

I nearly dropped my pencil.

"She's so young. Not much more than a child."

Young? My mother young?

"She called you Charlotte. It's a good name, Charlotte."

I turned and gave Sweet Pea more milk.

"I asked her to stay for tea," Beryl went on, "but she said she was tired and had to get home."

I remembered my mother standing by my door last night. I remembered the note this morning. "Be home."

Something smelled good. Hamburgers. My mother was at the stove. Her back was stiff. "I told you to be here early," she muttered.

I slid past her, washed my hands at the sink, took two plates and forks from the cupboard, and plunked myself down at the card table.

"You lied to me!" She whirled around, twisting her hands. "I finally got up my nerve and said to the boss, wasn't it nice that *my* daughter was friends with *his* daughter, and *he* said he didn't have any idea what I was talking about. It's a wonder I wasn't fired!"

I stared at my plate. I wanted to run out the door.

"My friend at the cannery, the one who gave you the clothes, she saw you. She told me where you *really* spend your days. Did you think you could keep it a secret? Don't you care what people think of us?"

You mean, what Mrs. Manning would think! I looked up. The lines were deeper down the sides of my mother's mouth.

She turned and slammed over another hamburger. "I went to that woman's place last night, to find out for myself, and the old thing kept smiling at me, asking me if I wanted some tea. I don't know what she has to smile about, crippled and alone as she is. What in the world do you want with her? I believe what I heard, that she's not right in her mind."

It was the most my mother had talked in a long time. She slapped the hamburgers onto the plates and sat down. A magazine lay on the table.

"You don't even know her."

"I know more than you, Miss. Why do you think I'm slaving like I do? So that I won't end up like her. So you'll have a better life than me!"

"But—"

"Don't you *but* me! The next thing I know, you'll be hobnobbing with the bums that come through here."

I sprang up and my chair fell over. "I don't know any bums!"

But she was hunched over the magazine, her lips tight, flipping the pages. I glimpsed a photograph of a kitchen all in white, with fluffy white curtains. A table was set with a white tablecloth, and on the table were the exact same pink-and-white dishes my dad had smashed.

The only sound was the slow *tick-tick* of the clock.
I left the table.
I stood by the stairs.
My mother didn't look up.

The next morning I went to the store to get something good for myself. Anything. I didn't care. I went to the store to steal.

11
Dad

The store fan whirred in the muggy air and flypaper swayed from the ceiling. "Happy Days Are Here Again" sang out from the scratchy-sounding radio on the counter. A fly buzzed onto the flypaper and stuck. Don was stacking cans of peas, and I made a grab for whatever I could reach.

Don turned around. Was he looking at me funny?

"Want something cold, Charley?" Don scooped ice chips from the cooler. "And, say, did you know better times are coming? Just heard President Roosevelt announce it again on the radio." He laughed, giving me a handful of ice. "Better times for the St. Louis Cardinals anyway."

The ice dribbled down my chin. The stolen bubble gum felt like it was boring a hole in my pocket. I didn't even *like* bubble gum.

*   *   *

Beryl sat under her tree, though it didn't give a bit of shade, and fanned herself with a yellowed newspaper. I stamped to the spigot, my mother's words going around in my head.

"Don't you care . . . don't you care what people think of us?"

I held up the hose, the water spurted out, and the words spurted hard and jagged from my mouth–"I hate her!"

Beryl reached out to me, but I twisted away.

The words kept coming. "She made my dad go! *She* should have gone!"

I dropped the hose and it curled like a snake.

"I used to beg her and beg her to stop screaming, but it never helped! And–and I hate him, too!" I was surprised, but I said it again. "I hate him! In two years he's sent me only three postcards . . . saying he missed me, was coming to see me. Cards from far away with no return addresses!"

My chest hurt. "He never knew me, either! He always wanted a boy, not *me*. And–and maybe I *was* always on his side, and maybe I *do* like to daydream, but I'm not like him, even though she thinks I am. I would never leave my own child!"

And then Beryl's arms were around me, and the front of her dress was wet from my crying. But she held me, and rocked me, and I stayed where I was. Sweet Pea climbed into my lap and I could hear his loud purring– and Beryl's heart beating under my cheek.

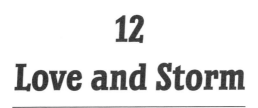

12
Love and Storm

The next day, under her tree, Beryl held out her arms and I walked into them. And I said, "I want to live with you."

I felt her tremble. "Your ma would not agree to that, Charley."

"She wouldn't care!"

Beryl shook her head.

I wanted to leave, to run away, but my feet wouldn't budge.

Beryl wiped her eyes with her apron. "I need my tea."

I found myself hoisting her up, helping her up the porch steps and into a chair. Maybe it was her son, and that was why I couldn't live with her. Maybe Tommy was coming back and he didn't want me.

I went into the kitchen. The tea jar was empty.

"Never mind," Beryl said. "We'll have mint tea instead.

Mint grows under the ladder in back of the house. You'll know it by its smell."

I'd known that already. I'd wheeled Beryl's old bike around the back. Now it stood deep in minty weeds.

As I knelt under the ladder, I wondered why it was always there, leaning up to the roof. I heard a growl and spun around. Across the side fence a big dog was baring its teeth at me, and a fat man was holding its leash. I'd seen the man sometimes when I'd sat on the fence watching the cows. He was the same man who'd honked at me that first day on the road. But why was he here, so close to Beryl's? And why was he stalking, moving back and forth? Like he was checking his side of the fence—like he was checking on me! I snatched up a few mint leaves and ran around the house to the porch.

In the kitchen, I dropped the mint in hot water. There was no sugar. And no graham crackers.

"There might . . ." Beryl said, "there might be some red raspberry jam in the root cellar."

I lifted the trapdoor. Looking down into the darkness—feeling the whoosh of cold air, inhaling the strong, wet-earth smell—it came to me. I'd *make* Beryl want me. She needed me to help her, didn't she? I'd make her need me so much, she'd never be able to get along without me.

I made my way down the slatted-wood boards. Every summer we'd grow a garden, cook up vegetable soup, sit on the porch, watch our butterflies being born. In the winter we'd light the woodstove, watch the flames, be cozy. . . .

There was a squeaking, a scurrying. Mice, I thought. Or—my throat closed—rats! I'd seen huge, slinky rats in the city.

I drew a shuddery breath and whispered, "Hello. Hello. It's only me."

The scurrying stopped. I kept talking while I groped with my hands, my eyes got used to the dark, and I found two dusty jars on a shelf. Still chattering to scare off the rats, I raced out of the cellar.

Safe on the porch, I proudly held out the jars of jam to Beryl, and she laughed and clapped her hands. But when I tried to tell her how scary it was in her cellar, all she did was look past me at the hazy sky. All she said was, "I can feel it in my bones, child. We're going to get our blessed rain."

Rain? What was she thinking? The heat pressed down. I sighed and went inside for spoons.

I served the tea with the jam, and remembered to give Sweet Pea his milk. Afterward I washed the cups and saucers and mopped the kitchen floor. Then I propped up the washboard in the sink and scrubbed the doilies from the front-room sofa. Beryl watched me march down the porch steps and hang them on the clothesline.

I searched for more ways to make myself useful. In the front room I arranged the stuffed animals in a row on the sofa. I got a rag and dusted whatever I could find. I went back to the porch and swept it clean. What else? I glanced at Beryl. "Can I comb your hair?"

Beryl nodded. "You are a good girl," she said, and wiped her eyes.

Behind her chair, I grinned. I could be a good girl, couldn't I. I concentrated on making a part on one side of Beryl's hair. I tried a part on the other side.

The vines began to rustle. Sweet Pea meowed, and one of the Walt-lizards skittered under the porch. Over and over, I combed Beryl's thin, white hair.

"Beryl," the question slipped out, "why do you think my parents got married at all?"

After a minute, she answered. "I don't know, child. Maybe they expected something different from each other than what they got. Being human and all." She held the teddy bear to her chest and mumbled, "Poor Leon."

I thought of the thin, mustached man in Beryl's photograph album.

"He was so sick," Beryl said. "And he grieved so long."

The sky darkened. A wind came up.

Beryl drew a long breath. "Smell that, child? That good, damp smell?"

"Beryl," I said in a rush, "do you think somebody like me could ever have a family? When she grows up, I mean. A real family of her own?"

Beryl turned. Her look was like light—so blazing, so full of . . . was it love?—that I had to bend my head. Was that . . . was that how my mother used to look at me?

70

The wind grew stronger. It blew our hair; it rattled the porch vines and flattened the grass. It shook the bare tree, making it creak and groan. Lightning flashed. We both jumped when thunder cracked.

"Run on home now," Beryl said.

"No, I want to stay with you."

We'd sit on the porch, be together in the storm, watch the lightning; I'd make tea. I had a funny picture in my head—the two of us dancing in the rain . . . .

Beryl said, "Your ma will want you home."

13
The Graveyard

The wind howled. Thunder crashed. Rain beat down on the roof. I felt under the cot for paper and pencil stubs. First I'd draw myself in Beryl's cellar fighting off gigantic rats, next I'd–

A tremendous clap of thunder made my room shake. Huddling under my blanket, I couldn't stop the pictures in my head: my mother pushing open the heavy cannery door, getting drenched–being struck by lightning!

The kitchen door opened, and I took a breath of relief. She started up my stairs.

I turned over, with my back to the door.

In the morning the road was muddy and full of holes. I skipped over them and saw the clear blue sky in the puddles. A million birds seemed to be chirping, a million raindrops sparkled on every leaf. I could hardly wait to tell Beryl the lizard and butterfly dream I'd had again.

And this time the strange dream had kept going. The tiny, golden butterfly inside the giant lizard's head had guided the lizard down through the darkness to a blue planet. And there—I could still see it—they began planting seeds in the ground.

At Beryl's gate, one of the Walt's tails disappeared into the weeds. Poor lizards. None of them were like the fantastic lizard in my dream.

Sweet Pea came swishing through the grass to greet me. And then I saw what the storm had done.

Beryl's tree—the one she sat under—her tree that she patted, that she talked to, the tree she'd planted when her son, Tommy, was born, lay splintered, like a fallen old man in the weeds.

Beryl stood on the porch, still in her thin, cotton night-gown. It didn't look very different than her flowered dress, except now I could see more of her stringy arms, with their folds of papery wrinkles. But instead of being stretched out to me, her arms were hanging loose at her sides.

"My boy is dead, Charley." Tears poured down her cheeks. "Dead, and buried in the ground."

I stared at her. Her boy? Tommy? Tommy who liked to eat watermelon? Who grew up playing with Don, the grocery man? Tommy whose toys were all over Beryl's house? Was it true? When did it happen? How? And why?

I walked slowly up the porch steps. My own arms felt stiff, but they found their way around Beryl's bony, thin body.

She sagged against me, her face pressed into my chest. And I held her. Like she'd held me when I'd cried. Like she'd held me.

Sweet Pea meowed and rubbed against us. Below us, a robin pulled up a worm. There was that humming in the air, like bees and billions of other insects were announcing they were here.

Beryl stopped shaking, and her sobbing slowed.

"We need a new tree, Charley." Her voice was muffled. "Our tree doesn't bear fruit anymore." She lifted her head. "We'll plant a peach tree next spring. Tommy likes peaches, you know."

I sat Beryl in her rocking chair. I went into the house and came back with the baby doll and the teddy bear. I put them both in her arms. Then I went back into the kitchen and put up water for tea.

The clouds glowed gold and orange. I stood outside the cemetery, afraid to go in. But the shadows were stretching longer, then longer still. Before I could change my mind, I made myself sidle through the gate.

I crept past the fallen-over gravestones, the moss-covered gravestones, the marble stone: IN MEMORY OF OUR BELOVED HUSBAND AND FATHER.

Something moved, and my breath caught. A bushy-tailed squirrel peered at me, then darted away.

The clouds changed, shifted into strange shapes, turned a deep red.

It was still. Very still. Too still.

The clouds turned purple. The light was almost gone. I waded through the weeds, up one row of graves and down another, trying to read the names.

The purple clouds faded. The gravestones stood dark against the sky.

I heard a slithering, a whispering, a shuffle of leaves. I felt a ghostly breath.

"It's only the wind."

My heart thudded. My own voice had scared me.

I made myself go to where the dark trees stood—to the far end of the graveyard.

I tripped over a flat stone. I bent down.

LEON STUBBS
1852–1924

Nearby, nearly hidden by purple flowers, was a smaller stone.

I could just make out the words.

THOMAS STUBBS
MAY 18, 1892–AUGUST 7, 1899

The purple flowers dipped and swayed.
A little boy.

14
Giving Food

I wanted to know about Tommy, to know why he died. I felt a stab whenever I looked at the fallen tree. But sitting on the straw, or in a rocking chair on the porch, Beryl talked about Tommy like she had before, as if he was still alive. I had to keep my discovery to myself.

Every morning I helped Beryl with whatever chores needed to be done. I didn't sit on the fence to watch the cows anymore, and I only saw the fat man and his dog from a distance. In the garden I felt under the straw, and if the ground was dry I dragged the hose over.

Butterflies flitted in and out of the spray. Sweet Pea purred around my ankles. One or another of the Walts sunned himself on the straw. I tried not to sprinkle the lizards. But I did water the weeds. They helped hide the fallen tree.

The seedlings grew so fast I could tell the difference from day to day. The vines grew curly, green tendrils. I curled the watermelon-vine tendrils around my finger, and I could almost feel them grab hold.

One day, Beryl touched a big orange flower. "This is a man squash flower," she told me. "The bees bring his pollen to the woman flower. And here," she touched another orange flower, "is a woman."

Under the woman flower I found a tiny green shape. "That's her baby," Beryl said. "She's growing her child."

I found more flowers with their new green squashes and I gave them extra water to help the little ones grow. And later, I drew a scrap paper picture of mother and father flowers smiling at each other, proud of their children.

Most afternoons, while Beryl napped, I walked to the river. Often I saw looking-for-work people in their camps among the trees; sometimes I saw kids. But they just stared at me, and the next day they were always gone. I was glad I didn't run into Maxine and Mikey. At their summer cottage, I guessed. One night, to make sure they were gone, I sneaked past their house. The house was dark.

At the river I searched for the best stones and pebbles. Together with interesting-shaped twigs, I arranged them under my tree. Beryl told me she knew that tree and gave me its name: weeping willow.

Every evening I walked back to Beryl's for supper and described the creatures I'd seen. She told me that the big, shiny blue flying bugs were dragonflies. The smaller, delicate ones were mayflies. Muskrat was the name of the sleek-haired animal that sometimes swam by me.

Some days I stopped to visit with Don. When the

news was on the radio, he told me President Roosevelt was still turning the country around, that things were looking up. When it was a baseball game, he'd tell me who was up to bat. Once I heard the galloping music of the Lone Ranger, but I didn't stay to listen. Instead I bought some chocolate bars to take to Beryl. And I didn't ask Don about the mail.

I ran out of paper. One day Don caught me poking through the store's trash barrel. He went into the back room and came out with an old Sears Roebuck catalog. "I guess this is better than nothing," he said. I thanked him. The pages would last me awhile. I still needed pencils.

Then one afternoon, when I was helping Don stack cans and boxes, the screen door banged open, and before I could duck, Mrs. Manning was inside.

"I see you have a little helper, Don," she said. She didn't seem to recognize me.

He gave a slight nod, said, "G'afternoon, Ma'am," and handed her the money-owed book. She ran her finger down the list. "It's too bad these people have to live the way they do, Don." She sighed. "I do feel sorry for them. But we can only do so much."

My teeth were grinding against each other till she left.

That night Don brought Beryl her groceries. She handed him some coins, but he shook his head. "I'm sorry, Beryl, this isn't nearly enough. You know the boss and his wife. The Mannings are back from their vacation, and she's checking the accounts as usual." He frowned. "And, as usual, I can't give you any more credit."

"Phooey on them!"

Beryl didn't pay me any attention. She gave back the bread, the half-dozen eggs, the milk, and the butter. She held onto the box of graham crackers.

After Don drove off I went out to the porch with the last drops of milk for Sweet Pea and found three big eggs—a present from Don. We scrambled them together with our first squash and beans, and our supper tasted so good I couldn't stuff it into my mouth fast enough.

"Don is a good boy," Beryl said. "I'm glad Tommy has him for a friend."

The garden kept growing, and hummed with bees. The tomato vines fell over the cucumber vines, the bean vines tangled in with the watermelon vines, and the tall stalks of corn stood straight up in the middle of it all. The tassels on the baby corn felt like silk.

We hadn't spotted any watermelons yet, but everything else was giving us food. I kept touching and sniffing, looking and finding. It was amazing that all this growing had come out of those tiny, leftover seeds. Amazing how the empty space was filling up. Amazing that *I'd* helped make it happen.

I exchanged some of our vegetables for milk and eggs at the store, and Beryl made me take lettuce, tomatoes, and cucumbers home for my mother. I left them on the card table to be sure she'd see them.

"This is the best garden in the whole world," I told Beryl.

"And my house. You like my house, too?"

"Yes!" I loved her run-down, slanty-stepped house.

Then one morning, as I was about to push open Beryl's gate, I heard, "Hey, Charley!"

I made a face. But I stopped. I didn't have anything against a little kid.

Mikey rolled up to me. "We're home from our vacation, Charley. Is Beryl Stubbs growing watermelons? Can we come in and see?"

"No. Besides, you said your mother wouldn't let you."

"Aw, she won't find out. Anyway, Charley, it was boring at the lake. Mom had company and we had to sit around in our good clothes the whole time!"

Maxine pedaled toward us and stopped.

"Isn't that right, Maxine?" Mikey squeaked. "And Mom made Maxine show off, singing stupid songs. Charley, can we see crazy Beryl Stubbs's garden? Maxine wants to see, too!"

I looked at Maxine. Was that a nod? She bit her lip and stared down at her new white shoes.

"You better go." I kept my voice flat and cold. "My crazy friend is waiting for me." I had one hand on the gate.

"Aw, Charley, if you let us come in, we'll let you come to the river with us. And catch frogs!"

I turned. Maxine was already riding away.

I stalked inside and slammed the gate so hard it nearly fell off its hinges.

15
Mother

The cannery was still going, day and night. When my mother climbed up my stairs at night, I pictured her work clothes dirty, her hair frizzy and undone, and the new lines down the sides of her mouth. When I tiptoed past her bedroom door on her rare Sunday off, I'd hear her toss; sometimes I'd hear her moan.

One afternoon, coming home for spoonfuls of peanut butter, I saw her soiled work dress crumpled over a chair. It looked so sad I had a strange feeling. I wanted to scrub it clean.

"Charlotte?" My mother's bedsprings creaked.

"Yes."

"Didn't you read my note this morning? I said I'd be home early."

I looked at the note on the card table.

"Come here."

I opened her bedroom door.

My mother sat in bed, staring at her chipped finger-nails. The dark roots of her hair showed; the lines on her face looked deeper.

"You're still spending your time with that pathetic old woman, aren't you?"

I clenched my hands. Didn't it mean anything that Beryl was giving her vegetables?

"I heard more about her. They say there was drunk-enness in her family—and something about another man, a bum. . . ."

I wanted to throw something at her.

"I've been thinking, Charlotte." She looked up for a second, then down at her hands. "I never told you how it was for me when I was your age. I had nothing, just a drunken father and a sick-to-death mother." Her hands began to twist together. "I escaped the first chance I got."

Married my dad, she meant.

"I'm not saying there's not some good in you being with the old woman. At least it keeps you safe and out of trouble. But I want better for you, and it's not too late."

I edged away.

"You can still make friends with the Manning girl. They're the kind of family I never had the chance . . ."

I was at the door.

"Charlotte . . ."

I ran out of the room.

"Charlotte, come back here!"

From outside the door, I yelled, "I'll go where I want, do what I want, and be with whoever I want to!"

16
Sunsets and Trouble

We sat on the porch waiting to see how the colors of the sunset would be—and eating spoonfuls of peanut butter I'd brought from home.

"Where do butterflies go at night?" I asked, scooping a big gob from the jar.

"Butterflies need to be warm to be able to fly," Beryl said, eating hardly any. "I don't know for certain, but I have a sense they find a safe leaf to hide under, fold up their wings, and go to sleep."

"What about lizards?"

"Lizards find the warmest place they can, too. And when summer is over, both the lizards and the butterflies will be gone."

"Where to?"

"Well," Beryl answered, "lizards dig under the ground for the winter, and butterflies fly to warmer places. But most butterflies, after they lay their eggs, are very tired and they die."

"I don't like that!" I wanted to ask more, but I saw that the sky was changing. I pointed up. "Look, Beryl! See how the color always gets more brilliant just before it's dark?"

Beryl squeezed my hand.

We watched the whole sky deepen to red.

"Beryl," I said, "can I ask you—"

She rocked. Her eyes seemed to be looking at something far away.

"Beryl, you know how you like the sky?"

She didn't answer.

I waited.

The red faded to purple. The shadows grew long. Sweet Pea settled in my lap.

"Beryl, can I ask you something?" And it spilled out. "Did you ever, I mean if you had the paints, did you ever make a picture of the sky?"

Beryl stopped rocking. She turned and gazed at me. "No, can't say I ever did."

"I know it's silly, Beryl," the words tumbled over each other, "but when I was little I had this idea that I'd paint the world's most beautiful picture of a sunset."

"That's not silly at all." Beryl squeezed my hand again. "You will, Charley. And when you do, will you make one brilliant cloud for me?"

I grinned. I'd even make the cloud look like her.

But then she was rocking again, her face closed. What was she thinking?

I waited. Crickets began to chirp. A ring of fireflies

danced over the garden. From across the fields, a whip-poorwill called. Sweet Pea's ears perked up.

Beryl's rocker stopped creaking. "Can I ask you something?"

"Yes! Of course!"

"I was thinking." Her voice was soft. "I was thinking we could make supper for your ma tomorrow night."

What? My mother here? With us?

"That way," Beryl reached over to me, "when she gets off work we can all eat together."

My eyes stung. I pulled away. "No!"

Beryl leaned back. She rocked.

I rocked, faster.

"Another time, then," Beryl said.

In her flowered dress Beryl looked like something strange and funny growing in the garden, and one hot day I held up the hose and watered her, let the water rain down on us both. We gawked at each other, soaked to the skin, our hair plastered and dripping. I sank down beside her, and we burst out laughing. Glancing up I saw Maxine and Mikey hanging on the gate. I stuck out my tongue at them and gave Beryl a sopping-wet hug. The kids sped away.

Beryl sat back. "My soul, child," she said, "now that you're good and watered, I've finally noticed it. You're growing as fast as the garden."

"And my feet are tough now, like yours!" It was true. I could walk barefoot almost everywhere. I stretched out my sun-browned fingers. "See? My hands are tough, too."

But the bigger and stronger I grew, and the bigger the garden became, the smaller Beryl seemed to get. She sat more and slept more. Often her face would crumple and turn white, and she'd gasp and clutch her side.

"What's wrong?"

"Just a stitch, child," she'd say. "Nothing to worry yourself with."

I'd make her tea, sit beside her, and keep my eyes on her face. And always she'd say, "You can leave me now, Charley. A little nap, and I'll be feeling just fine." So I'd feel better, too, and walk up the dirt road to the river.

Then one afternoon, when I was choosing pebbles for new designs, I heard their voices and slipped under my tree.

"I saw her." It was Mikey. Coming closer.

I pressed against the tree trunk.

"Are you sure?" It was Maxine. I could see her white shoes.

Mikey's freckled face poked through the leaves. "I *told* you she was here!" He lifted the branches and crawled in, with Maxine on her knees behind him.

"Hey," he squealed, "it's nice in here!"

Maxine stared at my pebble designs.

I glared at her. "This is a private place."

Mikey grinned. "We came to tell you, Charley. Beryl Stubbs's boyfriend is back."

"You're lying! Beryl doesn't have a boyfriend!"

"Yes she does!" Mikey's blue eyes sparkled. "Everybody knows it. Anyway, somebody saw him in Amesville today. I bet he just came back from everywhere in the whole country. When I grow up I'm going to be a hobo, too."

"Mikey!" Maxine looked horrified. "He never washes, his clothes stink, and Mom says he's really *bad*. There's no telling *what* old Walt's done!"

Walt? My stomach felt funny.

"And you know what, Charley?" Mikey piped up. "My mom says Beryl Stubbs' other old man, the one she was married to, was a drunk and was just as crazy as her!"

My face burned. "*She's* not crazy. *You* are! And go tell your stupid mother and father for me that they're crazy, too!"

The kids' jaws dropped.

"Now get out!" I grabbed a handful of stones.

They scrambled away.

"And stay out!" I threw the stones as hard as I could.

Stupid kids! Maybe they had a home and a mother and a father and supper together, but they didn't have butterflies or lizards or a garden. Or Beryl.

In the middle of the night, I awoke, my heart pounding and my breath coming hard. I dreamed I was back in the city, piling out of a boxcar with dozens of bums. My mother was there, twisting her hands and screaming, "You called my boss crazy! You made me lose my job!"

17
Crazy

The morning train came and went. The kitchen door banged shut. I pulled on my clothes and ran up the dirt road.

At the gate, Sweet Pea bounded through the grass and rubbed against me. Butterflies fluttered over the garden. But something was different, not right. Beryl didn't call out to me. She wasn't in her chair on the porch.

Then I saw her. She was in her flowered dress, face down on the straw.

I stood over her. I felt as cold as ice.

Beryl stirred and rolled over.

Oh! I put a hand to my heart and drew a shaky breath.

She smiled up at me. Pieces of straw stuck out of her hair.

"Beryl," I began, "I had a nightmare. It was–"

"Not now, child." She put a finger to her lips. "I am listening to the garden elves helping our garden to grow."

I glared down at her. I was ready to explode. Just when I needed her, needed to tell her, she was lying there being crazy—scaring me!

Beryl's lip quivered, and she turned her face away.

Oh, Beryl. I'm sorry, Beryl.

I lay down next to her and peered into our green jungle. A wind rustled the corn, then whispered in the vines. And I spied them. Not elves, but—and I yelled—"Tiny watermelons!"

I helped Beryl sit up, and we parted the leaves.

Beryl patted and stroked the small, round shapes, and said over and over, "Hello and welcome to you and you and you. I knew you'd grow for us. Now just lie back, my dears, and enjoy getting big and fat and juicy." She turned to me, chuckling. "Do you know what Tommy always says, Charley? He says that the slice of watermelon on his plate looks like a big, red smile."

I swallowed the lump in my throat. Then I bent and gathered more straw to make the baby watermelons soft beds.

In my head I saw Beryl on her knees planting the garden, saw her touching the tree. I heard her telling me about the butterflies, and about all of us—every single creature—being here together. I saw that look again, that look of love. I didn't care if Beryl *was* crazy. But then it came out. "Beryl, it's a lie, isn't it? You don't really have a bum, I mean a boyfriend who—"

"Walt?" Her eyes shone. "Is Walt back?"

I opened my mouth, then shut it. And then I told her

the truth, told her what I'd heard. She clasped my hands and squeezed them, and all of the wrinkles in her face turned up. I walked her to the porch, helped her into her chair, and went into the kitchen to make tea.

Searching for sugar far back in the cupboard, I found a pickle jar gleaming with pennies and quarters, nickels and dimes. I remembered Don shaking his head and Beryl giving back the groceries. She must be saving for something more important than food.

If the hobo saw her money, he might steal it.

I shoved the jar farther back in the corner.

18
The Roof

The next morning I had another thought. I'd better not leave Beryl by herself. I dressed and ran downstairs. My mother sat in the kitchen, drinking her coffee.

Was she fired? No, she had on her work clothes. Her purse lay beside her. So the kids hadn't told on me; that I said their folks were crazy. Hadn't told on me yet.

I held myself straight. "Beryl Stubbs invited me to sleep over at her house tonight," I lied. "She wanted me to ask you. But I don't care what you say. I'm going."

My mother didn't move, didn't speak. The cup in her hand stayed in the air.

Outside the morning train whistled. I ran out the door.

I watched the train roll by, first the passenger cars, then the boxcars. Two men in dirty overalls sat in an open doorway. When I was able to cross the tracks, I saw Don's truck turning off the dirt road. From the way he grinned and waved at me, I thought he must've been at

Beryl's already, even brought us a treat. But at morning tea time there was still no sugar, no graham crackers.

I lied again, telling Beryl that my mother said I could stay overnight.

"That was nice of your ma," she said.

I looked the other way.

I had another idea: I'd keep guard outside. "Can I spread out more straw," I asked, "and sleep by the garden?"

"That's the best way," Beryl said, "out in the open with the stars." She beamed. "And maybe the garden elves will pay you a visit."

While she dozed, I dusted and swept, picked squash and beans, and counted nine different shades of green in the garden. I patted the new watermelons and said "Hello" to each one.

One of the Walts pushed out of the straw. Slowly, I reached out a hand. The lizard didn't move. He let me touch his scaly-dry body for a second before he skittered away.

After our supper of fried beans and squash, Beryl told me to go around back. "Make sure," she said, "that the ladder is still leaning up to the roof."

"Why?"

"Walt will be coming."

I didn't move.

"Go on, Charley." Beryl's voice quavered.

I went and came right back. "It's there."

"Now," she said, "let's go up. We don't want to miss the first star, do we?"

Did she really mean to climb to the roof? She could barely walk up the porch steps. "Beryl–"

"Walt and I have sat on the roof to see the first star most every summer since Leon's been gone." Her mouth was set. "And I am going to sit there now."

I counted fifteen rungs on the ladder. But Beryl was so skinny it wasn't too hard to push her, slowly and steadily, from behind. With every step the sky grew darker. With every step Beryl gasped, trying to catch her breath.

By the time we made it onto the roof, the first star wasn't the only star out.

"That's all right." Beryl lowered herself onto the shingles. "We're here."

Below us, the fireflies flickered. The crickets started up.

"I wish I may . . ." Beryl's eyes were closed. "I wish I might . . . have the wish . . ."

I lay back. Above me the huge curve of night slowly filled with a million twinkling lights. I felt as if I was floating up to them–up, up into the deepness of space. I held fast onto the roof and looked over at Beryl. I had a wish, too.

I'd push her up the ladder every night if she wanted, if only it was just her and me. If only nobody would ever be allowed on the roof with us, especially not a bum.

The gate creaked open.

"It's Walt." Beryl sat up.

"Walt," she called, "we're up here on the roof."

19
Walt

A beat-up, wide-brimmed hat. A beak of a nose, a whiskery chin. An old man hoisted himself onto the roof. I edged away.

The old man put his big arms around Beryl, and the two of them stayed that way for a long time.

"My sweetheart." His voice was hoarse. "I missed the first star again."

"Never mind." Beryl tweaked his ear. "You're here with me now."

Even in the dim light I could tell that the old man's eyes were watery.

They sat quiet, holding hands. Then, Beryl said, "I didn't know if you were alive or dead, Walt."

The old man hung his head.

"Not even a postcard."

"Beryl, you know me. Anyhow, I've been north again. This time I had a hankering to get to Alaska. Almost made it. But," he gave a heavy sigh, "guess I'm too old. I *felt* old just now, climbing your ladder."

Beryl reached up and stroked his face.

I shifted, had to cough.

"Oh, my, how could I forget." Beryl giggled. "Walt, I want you to meet my friend, Charley."

"Well!" he said. "What d'ya know!" He grinned, showing big teeth, one missing in front. I held myself back, but he reached over and grabbed my hand. "Glad to know any friend of my girl here."

He turned to Beryl again. "I knew I had to see you, sweetheart." He bent, his hat hiding his eyes. "It's been a year."

Beryl laughed. "And it's exactly sixty-five years, Walt. I came here to work in the fields when I was sixteen. It's sixty-five years this summer since we met."

"You don't say!" Walt kissed her wrinkly cheek. "Well, that's right, isn't it. You were the prettiest little thing in the whole county, and I was that dashing, handsome young fellow. Seems like only yesterday."

Something huge and shadowy floated over us, and I clutched the nearest arm.

"Owl," Walt said, and laughed.

I snatched my hand away.

The old man didn't seem to notice. "Beryl, I thought of you. Especially when I was by the tracks, or in a box-car, and someone brought out a banjo and we hollered out songs all night."

While they talked, I opened the holes in my nose and

sniffed. Walt smelled sweaty, like unwashed clothes, but mostly he had a wild, smoky smell, like outdoor fires.

From somewhere a night train hooted. Softly, Beryl started to sing. Walt chuckled and joined in, louder.

> Down by the old mill stream,
> Where I first met you . . .
> You were sixteen,
> My village queen,
> Down by the old mill stream.

They sang it over and over, holding onto each other, and I couldn't help seeing the picture they made: him big and gnarly, and her gnarly, too, but small as a bird. And the way she touched him, the way he looked at her . . . was that how it was supposed to be between a man and a woman?

Walt began another song, then Beryl took a turn. They sang "Row, Row, Row Your Boat" and "I Love You Truly." They sang "Take Me Out to the Ball Game" and "Keep the Home Fires Burning." They sang song after song. Even "Twinkle, Twinkle Little Star" sounded shiny and new with the way they harmonized.

I looked up, blinked, and looked again. There was a lizard in the sky, and he was made out of millions and millions of stars. "Does anybody see a lizard in the Milky Way?" I asked.

"A lizard?" Walt laughed.

My face got hot. I shook my head. The lizard melted into the shining blanket of the Milky Way.

Out of nowhere, Beryl said, "I feel lucky."

Walt and I both turned. For a minute, in the starlight, Beryl looked as young as the young Beryl in her photograph album.

Walt stared. Then "Beryl . . . " He bent and cleared his throat. "I've brought you a new song, Beryl."

He began to sing.

"This little light of mine, I'm gonna let it shine, this little light . . .

"I learned this one from a guy around a fire," Walt said. "Let's sing it together."

All at once my mother was in my head. She was climbing up the ladder; she was on the roof with us. It was an impossible picture, but I couldn't make her go away.

I saw us all very small; we were in the deepness of space; we were floating with the stars—and we were all singing.

> This little light of mine,
> I'm gonna let it shine.
> Let it shine, let it shine,
> Let it shine.

20

The Wish

The night air grew chilly. Walt helped Beryl down the ladder, and they stood at the bottom looking up at me.

I wanted to keep hanging onto the roof, wanted to keep feeling the deepness. "Can I stay up here?"

"No, child," Beryl said. "We want you down here with us."

"I can set you up to sleep outside, Charley," Walt said.

I remembered that I was going to sleep in the garden anyway. I climbed down, Walt lifted me off the ladder, and we all went around the house to the porch.

Walt turned on the light in the kitchen. A moth followed him in where the screen door was torn.

He came outside with the tea. I brought out the last of the raspberry jam.

"Charley found the jam, Walt," Beryl said. "You know how Tommy loves my preserves."

Walt held tight onto her hand. A whippoorwill called. From across a field came the answer, "Poor will . . . poor will . . ." And we sat in the soft darkness, listening to the callings and the answerings and the rustlings in the night.

Walt brought blankets from the house, made a bed on the straw, and tucked the blankets around me. Beryl smiled down at me, and Sweet Pea padded over and curled under my arm. Then Beryl said, "Good night, sleep tight," and I watched Walt's big shape help her small one walk up the porch steps.

The rocking chairs began to creak. As if I was standing off to the side, I saw myself lying with Sweet Pea in our good-smelling garden, the stars above me, and the two old people on the porch. The scene was like one of my daydreams. But daydreams don't stay. You have to wake up from them. This was real.

"Remember, Beryl?" Walt was chuckling. "Remember the year I came back to visit you, and I ate so many apples off your tree that I got a bellyache?"

It was easy to feel that I was with a loving grandma. As for Walt, I'd wait and see. But maybe, just for now, I could make believe that I was with a grandfather, too, could pretend we were a family. I saw them sitting around the table on the porch, saw myself coming out of the kitchen carrying a big pot of homemade vegetable soup, the best soup they'd ever tasted.

"Your garden looks good, Beryl," I heard Walt say. "How about one of these days you and Charley make me your good vegetable soup?"

My eyes popped open. A light streaked through the dark.

A shooting star.

I closed my eyes and wished.

21

The Pickle Jar

The sun was hot on my face. I opened my eyes. Near me a cucumber vine was showing off its prickly new cucumbers. A new watermelon was peeking out from its cover of leaves. A blanket was under me, and another was on top. The air smelled sweet.

Now I remembered. The old man, Walt, had spread out the blankets and tucked them around me. I sat up and looked around. Walt was near the side fence, dragging off the fallen tree's branches. I pulled straw from my hair–tried to smooth my hair down.

Beryl was in her rocking chair on the porch, her bed quilt over her knees.

Then, next to me, I saw a brown paper package.

I carried it to the porch and asked, "What's this?"

Beryl's eyes crinkled. "It's for you."

"For me?" Slowly I untied the string and undid the paper.

Inside was a box of pencils, and two real painting brushes—one big and one small. They tickled when I touched them to my cheek. There was a thick pad of pure white paper. Best of all, there was a set of paints with five colors: magenta red, aqua blue, yellow, white, and black.

I hugged them to me and couldn't get out a word.

"Don went to Amesville," Beryl said, "and got what he could. But I know an artist needs green and orange and purple, too. An artist needs all the colors."

I found a tray Beryl said I could use and squeezed out a bit of color from each tube. I dipped the small brush into water and mixed the red with the yellow to get orange, the yellow with the blue to get green, and the red with the blue for purple. I added white to some. I added black to others.

"Beryl," I shouted, "I can *make* almost all the colors!"

The colors all ran together in the middle. I swished the big brush into the puddle, and it came out brown. I decided it was a good brown. Like the good ground in our garden.

Then the thought came. Paints and brushes and good paper cost money.

I got up, went into the house, and looked in the cupboard. The pickle jar was there, but it wasn't where I'd hidden it. And it was empty.

Beryl had used up her money for me.

22
The Question

By the second day I decided it wasn't so bad having Walt with us. He washed and shaved clean, and laughed when his big chest popped the buttons on Leon's shirts.

Every day he did repairs. He patched up the screen door, fixed the gate, and nailed whatever was coming apart. One morning we both climbed the ladder to the roof, and he let me help him hammer down the falling-off shingles.

Walt pointed his finger to the big field next door, then to the woods beyond. "When I was a boy," he said, "I took a shortcut through there to one of my hangouts, a real dilly of a marsh. It's where one of our rivers winds around–there's rivers all over this area, you know. The railroad tracks head up that way, too." That got him started telling me about the boxcars and the campfires, about the freedom of the big spaces out there, some-where far.

I could see him out there, riding the rails, sitting around a dilly of a campfire–singing songs with my dad!

"You heard about me, haven't you, Charley?"

I stared at him. My mind was still out there–somewhere. . . .

Walt squinted at me and said it again. "You heard about me?"

I shook my head.

"No? Well, one thing, you know that Beryl and me go back a long ways, even before Leon." His bushy eyebrows scrunched together. "You know about Leon?"

I shook my head again.

"No? Well–anyhow. . ." Walt's eyes were watery, but his mouth made a kind of grin. "You should've seen us. Beryl and me were the cat's pajamas together."

I could see Walt, young and handsome, rowing Beryl, sixteen, the village queen, out in a boat on the river.

"But she got away from me, Charley. She married Leon."

Walt turned and pounded down a loose shingle.

"That time when I stayed away too long."

Walt fixed the porch swing, and the three of us swung back and forth, balanced perfectly, with me in the middle holding Sweet Pea. Once I spied Maxine and Mikey by the fence. I sat up in the swing and yelled, "Well, well, what have we here?" just like their football-star father had yelled at me. Walt said, "I guess you know those kids?" And Beryl said, "Let's invite your nice friends in."

"No!" I leaned back so hard we nearly tipped over. When I looked again, they were gone.

Every day I stationed myself on the porch with my art supplies and made pictures for Beryl. Feeling the shapes of things with a pencil, or splashing on color, I didn't have to fume or stew; my mind didn't have to keep going around in circles. I felt like the garden, quietly stretching out and blooming, and I didn't ever want to stop. I wasn't afraid of running out of paper, either. Don said he'd save me whatever paper he could at the store.

"And maybe later," he said, "you'll be able to buy your own supplies. Maybe–just maybe–I could hire you to help me out at the store."

Maybe, I thought. But not if Maxine decided to tell her folks about me.

Working on a picture of Sweet Pea asleep with his paws in the air, I looked up to see Walt hauling over the old bike.

"Beryl said it's yours." Walt grinned at me. "Still rusty, but it'll go now, almost as good as new."

I wanted to hug him. My arms were getting used to hugging.

"I–I don't know how to ride a bike," I said.

Walt didn't bat an eye. I wanted to hug him even more.

"Tell you what," he said. "I got more chores. We'll practice riding tomorrow."

I looked closely at Walt, at his brown, creased face, at

his beak of a nose, at his bald head fringed with white. The blue paint was already laid out, and I knew how to make the right brown. "Will you sit still for me, Walt?" I asked. "For your picture?"

"You gonna make me an old lizard?"

"Yes." I giggled. He looked more like an old eagle.

"Hold on a minute." Walt clumped into the house. He came back out wearing his hat and sat himself in a rocker, his back straight and with his eyes looking straight ahead. "The chores can wait. You can start now."

I made him the captain of a ship—put a captain's hat on his head and a blue sky behind him. I thought for a minute, then drew him in Alaska, steering his ship between giant rainbow-colored icebergs. As a final touch, I put a big eagle on his shoulder.

I gave him his portrait. "This one is for you, Walt," I said.

Walt held it for a long time. "I thank you." His eyes teared up. "For the honor." He handed the drawing back to me. "You keep it, Charley. To remember me by."

To remember him by? He wasn't going off again, was he? He was too old. He'd even said so himself.

Beryl, sitting in her rocker, didn't seem to hear. She just kept beaming, kept saying over and over that she'd never known a true artist before. She had Walt take down the old magazine pictures and tack up mine: the cows and Sweet Pea; the monster tomato worm that made me scream when I reached in for a tomato; leaves that looked like elephants and whales and giraffes; and the inside designs of vegetables when you slice them open.

I knew it was silly, but I showed one of the lizards my picture of the giant lizard in the sky. And—I could have been imagining it—but I think he smiled to see himself made out of stars.

Looking at a drawing of two frogs leaping out of the water, Walt said, "I can tell you like these critters," and I found myself telling him about Maxine and Mikey catching frogs at the river. "You don't say!" Walt chuckled. "I used to catch frogs myself. I'll take you sometime."

I painted a sunset with Beryl as a beautiful, red-colored cloud, like I'd promised myself I would. I wanted it to be the best picture of all. When I was satisfied, I propped it against a porch step and stood back. Something was missing. Then I saw what it was. I drew a little cloud boy in Beryl's arms.

Beryl gazed at her picture. And suddenly, I got afraid. I saw that it could be a picture of heaven; it could be Tommy being dead. But Beryl just laughed and clapped her hands and said, "That's just how it is!"

"Hang it opposite my bed, Charley," she told me, "so I can see it every morning when I wake up. In fact, I'm going to have a nap right now."

I tacked up the painting and helped her into bed. I took hold of her hands. They were cold; I could feel all the tiny bones. I rubbed and rubbed her hands between mine.

"You want to know something, child?"

"What?" I tucked a pillow behind her head.

"This summer was my best garden ever."

"Really?"

"Know something else?"

I covered her with the quilt. "What?"

"I feel happy. So happy you came to me. And happy . . . " I had to lean close to hear her, "to know that you are a good friend to Tommy."

Her eyes closed. Even in her sleep, Beryl smiled.

I went out to the porch, pulled Walt from a rocking chair, and dragged him down the steps to the garden.

Standing among the corn plants, I asked him, "How did Tommy die?"

23
The Mirror

Walt scowled at me, then at the ground. "Beryl was working at the cannery," he mumbled, "and Leon was supposed to be watching the boy. But that drunken souse lay on the sofa watching the *bottle*. Sucking it dry!"

He coughed and cleared his throat. "Tom was an adventuresome little guy, always poking around, always exploring. And he liked the river." His voice sounded heavy. "Beryl found him downstream from here."

"Oh, no!"

I could hear Tommy scream, could see him swept under the water. My throat closed. I saw Beryl finding him, his little white shirt floating around him—saw her lifting him up, saw her carrying his small, dead body back home.

"Leon nearly went crazy afterward, drank even more. But she stayed with him, even after that. He lost most of his land, drove people away, and *still* she took care of him. And when he finally kicked the bucket—when was it?—ten, twelve years ago?—no friends were around, nobody. And me being gone and all. . . ." Walt's shoulders sagged. "But you know Beryl," he said. "She never quits. She keeps on."

He took off his hat and rubbed a big hand over his head. "Charley, you don't know much about me. After she married Leon I got hitched, too; tried to settle down but—hell . . ." He looked away. "I guess I'm what you'd call a bum, always on the move, never sticking around where I'm needed. At the bottom of it, Charley, I'm no better a man than Leon."

"No, Walt . . ."

But then I sank into my own thoughts. My dad hadn't stuck around, either.

"It wasn't so long ago that Beryl kept chickens and a cow on what was left to her—this measly half-acre. She was strong then, grew a bigger garden; she sold half her vegetables and canned the rest, all the while humming and singing."

He pulled out a torn, gray hankie and swiped at his eyes. "Maybe it was only to keep up her spirits, but Beryl always did love to sing."

His leathery, old face brightened. "And her baking!" He smacked his lips. "The best apple pie. And Charley, you should've seen us dance!"

He put his arm around me and twirled me around the garden. The cows next door watched us. The butterflies fluttered around us. Sweet Pea scooted out from under our feet.

"I predict you'll be as good a dancer as Beryl." Walt huffed to catch his breath. "And you know what, Charley? When you smile, you're just as pretty."

I blushed. I went up the porch steps, tiptoed into Beryl's bedroom, and looked in her oval mirror. My hair had grown out; it was curling up at the edges, and I saw glints of red and gold in the brown.

I smiled. How crazy! I *was* pretty.

24
The Marsh

"**Y**ou painted this picture?"

It was morning. My mother was in my room, staring at Walt's portrait.

I nodded, thinking she'd ask me where I got the paints.

"Who is he?"

"Nobody." I kept my eyes on Walt.

"Wait a minute! I know who he is. He's that bum people are talking about. The one with the old woman."

"You're wrong! You don't know! You're *wrong*!"

"I was thinking about visiting Mrs. Stubbs–to thank her for the vegetables, pay her somehow, for keeping you. I have to admit you've filled out, look healthier, and I'm glad. But not this! Not a bum!" She threw me my blouse and blue jeans. "Get dressed, Charlotte. I'm afraid I have to find someone who'll keep an eye on you."

Who? A baby-sitter? Another Mrs. Krenkel? "That's what you think!" I pulled on the clothes and ran down the stairs.

"Come back here!" Her voice was a shriek. "It's for your own good!"

I ran across the railroad tracks and onto the paved road. I knew she wouldn't come after me. *Nice* people didn't scream outside of the house. *Nice* people didn't chase after their kids! I saw someone hurrying toward town—a man wearing a wide-brimmed hat and a plaid shirt, the shirt Beryl had given him. Leon's shirt. I raced after him.

"Walt!" I yelled.

He turned and looked at me, then back toward Valley Junction. He kept walking, but not as fast. I caught up with him.

"Walt, where're you going?"

He gave me a sidelong glance from under his hat. "Oh, just out trampin' a little."

The train came chugging up the tracks. We stood watching the passenger cars file past, then the boxcars. From the top of a boxcar, ragged-looking men looked silently down at us. The train hooted and clanged past.

"Tell you what, Charley." Walt's eyes were clamped on the caboose. "Let's you and me have a little adventure."

Black smoke drifted back. The caboose wobbled away.

"We'll get a bucket at Beryl's place." Walt led me back toward the dirt road.

At Beryl's gate, I saw Maxine and Mikey riding toward us.

"Are those the frog catchers?" Before I could stop him, Walt yelled, "All frog lovers, gather 'round!"

They skidded to a dusty stop.

Walt knelt on the road with his arm around me. "I'm willin' and able right this minute," he said in a loud, mysterious whisper, "to take you all to my secret marsh."

The kids were goggle-eyed.

"This way." Walt opened the gate.

Without a glance at his sister, Mikey wheeled in his bike. And—I couldn't believe it—Maxine followed him. I stomped past them, peered into Beryl's bedroom window and looked daggers at the kids. "Keep away from the house!" I snapped. "My crazy friend is still asleep."

Around the back, Walt had one foot on the fence.

Maxine screeched, "We can't go in there! That's Mr. Crain's field!"

"Yeah!" Mikey echoed. "He's got a mean guard dog!"

I thought of the fat man and his dog.

Walt grinned. "Don't worry, kids." He puffed up his chest, and Mikey giggled. "I'm bigger than old Crainy. Besides, I knew him when this land didn't belong to him. Don't worry, he's all bluff."

Walt hauled himself over the fence and strode ahead, calling behind him, "Watch out for the cowpies!"

I climbed over after Walt. The cows walked toward me. They were practically on top of me. They were enormous.

I forced myself to turn my back on the cows, made myself face the kids and say, "If you're scared you can go on home."

"Wait for me! I'm coming!" Mikey scrambled after me.

"Mikey, come back here! Don't you dare go in there without me." Maxine followed Mikey over the fence and grabbed his arm.

The cows put down their big heads and began to munch. I made myself walk around them.

We caught up with Walt across the field, standing by a barbed-wire fence. "I know Crainy owns cattle now," he said, scratching his bald head, "but why in thunder does he need barbed wire?" He grinned and winked at us. "We ain't gonna let a little bob-wire stop us."

He found a place where the wire was loose and helped us crawl under. On the other side, a sign warned, KEEP OUT!

We stuck close behind Walt.

In the woods we had to go single file. A blue jay squawked at us. A squirrel scolded. The ground got soft and mushy under our feet.

And Walt announced, "We're here."

25
The Attack

Tall reeds and cattails stood in the mud around the edges. Oily bubbles rose to the surface. We lined up on the bank and stared into the dark, swampy water of the marsh.

"This is the place I told you about, Charley," Walt said. "Where I used to come when I was a boy."

From the top of a tall pine tree a flock of red-winged blackbirds swooped down to the water. A mosquito landed on my arm. I slapped at it and saw a bright red blob.

A dragonfly buzzed over the marsh. A yellow butterfly drifted by. Walt wiped his sweaty forehead with his sleeve and unbuttoned his shirt.

Mikey gawked at the white hair on Walt's chest.

"Beryl told me that dragonflies live only for a summer," I said, taking Walt's arm. "Most butterflies, too. But Beryl," my voice was loud, "Beryl who knows practically everything there *is* to know, also told me that butterflies leave hundreds of eggs behind."

"Really?" Mikey squeaked. "I want to see them! My sister does, too! Don't you, Maxine?"

Maxine stared at the butterfly, gave a slight nod and kept her eyes on the mud.

A gigantic green shape plopped into the marsh. Then another. Then another. The kids' eyes nearly popped. I think mine did, too.

Walt chuckled. "Yep, the bullfrogs are still here."

I glanced sideways at Maxine, kicked off my sneakers, and stepped into the brown water. They didn't know I'd never stepped in muck before, had never even seen a cow—or a river—till we moved to Valley Junction. Maxine's squeal was worth the squishing and sucking around my ankles.

Walt shed his boots and rolled up his pants, then waded in and handed me the bucket. Another huge frog dove in. Mikey hollered, "Let's get him!" and pulled off his shoes. Finally Maxine placed her socks and shoes far back on the bank, made a disgusted face, and tippy-toed into the water.

I spotted another bullfrog. Slowly, stealthily, holding the bucket out in front of me, I sneaked up on it. It dove under the water. Another frog surfaced, but before I could corner it, it leaped a giant leap away.

Then, right in front of me, I spotted the biggest frog of all. I motioned to Maxine and Mikey. They got behind it to cut off its escape, I crept closer, and, without even looking, the frog sprang straight into the bucket. We were soaked and splattered with mud, but we had it!

I gritted my teeth, reached in with both hands, and pulled out the bullfrog, bigger than Walt's foot, clammy-cool and spotted, with long webbed feet. I could hardly hold onto its slippery white stomach.

Maxine squealed.

Walt chuckled. "Good job." I forced myself to grin.

Mikey jumped up and down. "I want him! I want to take him home!"

"Well, you can't, so stop it," Maxine said. "He'll just die at home and you know it."

Silently, I agreed. Maybe Maxine wasn't always so dumb after all.

The giant frog squirmed in my hands. I dropped it back in the water and wiped my hands on my pants.

"OK, kids," Walt was saying, "time to get you home."

We left the marsh with dozens of bullfrogs garrumph-ing us good-bye. I could tell they were grateful we were finally leaving them alone.

Behind me, I heard Mikey say, "You should see your shorts, Maxine. You're gonna get it when we get home." And from Maxine, "Mom's too fussy! Besides, I can do what I *want* with my own clothes!"

I began to sing, and with a voice like a bullfrog, Walt boomed it out with me. "This little light of mine, I'm gonna let it shine—" Mikey caught on to the words and sang along. I listened. Maxine was singing, too. And through the trees, parading first in line and swinging my arms, I shouted out the song even louder.

We marched to the KEEP OUT sign, crawled back under the barbed wire, and tramped through the field toward Beryl's house. We were almost to the fence when I heard the bark.

Mr. Crain was coming at us. "So you're back, you lousy bum! Get off my property!" The dog growled and strained on the fat man's leash.

Maxine stood paralyzed.

Mikey ran behind Walt. Walt grinned.

I grabbed Walt's hand. "Come on!"

Walt snickered. "Why're you getting so hot under the collar, Crainy? You'll catch apoplexy if you don't calm down."

"You shiftless good-for-nothing!" The man was almost on us.

"Walt!" I tugged. "Let's *go!*"

"You and all the other homeless bums! We'll soon be rid of you! You *and* your crazy old woman!"

I spun around. My head felt like it was on fire. "Shut up!" I rushed at the fat man and butted him hard in the stomach.

Mr. Crain's feet went out from under him. He fell backward, jerking the dog on top of him, and they collapsed in a swearing, snarling tangle.

Walt yelled, "Run!"

Maxine and Mikey sprinted to the fence.

Mr. Crain lay on his back, cursing, "You lousy, no-good kid!"

I thought I heard Mikey shout, "Run, Charley!"

Walt half dragged, half carried me over the fence.

Mikey swung my hand back and forth and danced around me.

Walt threw back his head and let out a giant guffaw.

And Maxine.

First she gaped at me.

Then she let out a giggle.

Then Maxine was laughing, too.

26
The Leap

I tossed and turned. I got twisted up in my sheet. Over
and over I heard myself scream, heard Mr. Crain curse,
heard the dog snarl. Over and over I saw Maxine's
staring, white face. At last, near morning, I was able to
remember Walt's whoop, Mikey's dance, and Maxine's
surprising giggle.

"I can't bear it!" My mother was shaking me.

I curled up in a ball.

"You could have been arrested, Charlotte! Trespassing
on a private field with that bum you're such pals with!
They're going to catch the bum and put him in jail for
attacking Mr. Crain!"

"What?" I sat up. "Walt didn't hit him! I did!"

She didn't seem to hear.

"And Walt's not a bum! It's none of your business,
anyhow!"

"*None of my business?*" Her face turned splotchy.

"I work like a dog to keep a roof over our heads while you're running around with bums, and it's none of my business? What's just as bad, you can bet the Mannings will blame *us* for their kids being there! They say Mrs. Manning's in shock."

I imagined Mrs. Manning's face puffy, her perfect curls mussed up. I pulled up the sheet to cover my grin.

My mother ripped it away.

"Stop it!"

She took hold of my arm. "I have no choice. I can't let you be taken in by another—by a no-good like . . ." Her hold on me tightened. "I've already called Mrs. Krenkel. You'll stay with her until I decide what to do."

What was she doing to me? What was she thinking? That I'd go back to the city? Leave Beryl? And Walt? And the garden? I struggled to get away. "You can't make me!"

Her grip was like iron.

I gave up and let her get me dressed.

My thoughts raced. I'll catch her off guard outside and run like I did before. She won't run after me, and even if she does, she won't be able to catch me. I'll hide out at Beryl's house—in Beryl's cellar. . . .

She dragged out my suitcase and hustled me down the stairs.

They'll bring me food—my mother will move back to the city—Beryl and Walt will adopt me. . . .

I was so busy scheming that I didn't hear the train whistle. By the time I realized what was happening, my mother had me across the tracks and was flagging down the train. And before I could wrestle free she was shoving me on the train, pushing money and the suitcase at a conductor and shouting, "Mrs. Krenkel will meet you at the main station! I'll come as soon as I can!"

Her face disappeared. The conductor sat me down. The train was moving!

I rubbed my eyes and stared at the high-backed seat in front of me. How had it happened? Was this a nightmare? It was like watching a movie where you blink your eyes and miss the important part.

In the seat opposite me, a man was reading a newspaper. Cigarette smoke hung in the air.

Then the conductor was back, smiling down at me. "So you're off on a trip by yourself, eh, little lady?"

I didn't answer. He shook his head and left the suitcase on the seat next to mine.

I scrunched my face against the train window. Through the trees I saw gray sky and a glimpse of gray river. The wheels clickety-clacked, the train swayed. The river rushed by the other way. I slumped hopelessly in my seat.

Suddenly cornfields appeared, and I jumped up. I was going to harvest the corn today. And squash and carrots and beans. Don was bringing onions and potatoes. We were going to surprise Beryl and Walt with homemade vegetable soup today!

The train took a curve and I fell back. I clutched the suitcase and kept my eyes on the fields. I prayed there would be another stop, another town before we got to the city. I'd get off, walk back.

Wet drops began to splatter on the window. The outside misted over. Rivers of rain flowed down the glass.

The train kept swaying, shaking, rattling—it seemed for hours. With my arm I wiped the clouded-up window. The landscape had changed into unfamiliar hills and thick forests.

Then the chugging slowed. The train gave a jerk—and stopped.

Where were we? I didn't see a town or even a train stop. I peered down the train aisle.

"Don't worry, little girl," the man with the newspaper said. "They always check the brakes when they get here."

Beryl needed me. I had to get back. But if my mother found out. . . . I'd run away with Walt, the two of us in a boxcar; it would serve my mother right if I disappeared forever! But what about Beryl? Could we take her with us? No, we'd have to come back later in the dead of night, gather her up and . . .

My head felt dizzy.

The whistle sounded, and the train gave a jerk.

I stood. My legs shook. I squeezed the suitcase to my chest.

Another jerk. I lost my balance, nearly fell.

The train began to move.

I stumbled down the aisle to the open door.

Before the train gathered speed, I leaped.

27
The River!

I rolled away from the tracks. My suitcase landed near me. My knees and elbows were skinned. But I was still in one piece.

The caboose disappeared around a bend.

The steady drizzle made mud out of the gravel, made the tracks slick and shiny. I opened the suitcase, pulled out my sweater, and tugged it on. The only sound was the whispery patter of the rain.

I did the only thing I could do. I started back the way the train had come.

The ground fell steeply away alongside the tracks; there was barely enough space for walking, and it was hard to keep going with the suitcase slapping against my leg. My sweater got damp, then soggy, and my hair hung in strings. Wet and miserable, I stumbled on.

I heard something–a faint roar. Behind me. A train! I turned in a fright and tripped over a railroad tie. The suitcase pulled me off balance. Before I knew it I was halfway down a gully, ankle-deep in mud.

I dug in with my fingers, trying to claw my way up to the tracks, but only came away with handfuls of gravel. I couldn't get a foothold or a toehold, and I kept slipping down. At last I just clung to the hill and sobbed.

The roar was in my ears. I twisted my head and looked over my shoulder. Below me I saw my suitcase. I let myself slide backward.

The roar grew louder. I saw a shine of something farther down. Water. The noise must be rushing water. The river!

I yanked the suitcase out of the stickery bushes and slid down the hill. I found myself in a tiny clearing on the shore. All around me were tall trees tangled with vines and thick hedges of blackberry bushes.

The river was narrow here. It rushed over big rocks and boulders; it foamed and churned and leaped up. The noise was deafening.

I tried to think. From the train I'd seen the current going the other way, back toward Valley Junction. I was sure of it. So upstream was the way I'd need to travel to get back to Beryl's. I'd hide among the trees in case anyone came looking for me. I'd wait by the bridge, and when it got dark I'd just walk down the dirt road. Beryl and Walt would be on the porch—we'd have tea and graham crackers. . . .

Finding the river was lucky. I could see the policemen scratching their heads, saying, "That girl's disappeared into thin air." But—what about Mrs. Krenkel? She'd be waiting at the station. When I didn't show up she'd call the cannery. I mashed handfuls of juicy berries into my mouth to blot out my mother's anxious face.

I put out my hand to find a way through the bushes. With a cry I pulled it back, bleeding. I could never get past the wall of thorns. The other side of the river looked more open, but how could I get across the angry water?

I took hold of a vine, but I knew I could never swing across the river like Tarzan, or even Jane. Until I saw an opening on this side I'd have to travel by stepping from one rock to the next just off the shore.

The rain had stopped and a pale sun was spreading through the gray. I knocked the gravel from my shoes, shoved my shoes and my sweater into the suitcase, and gripped a wet rock with my toes. The weight of the suitcase made me teeter, but I balanced myself and took a step.

Another step. So far, so good.

Another big rock. Then another. I set one foot on the next smaller rock to make sure it would hold me. But it was mossy. I slipped, lost my grip on the suitcase and it splashed into the water. My heart in my mouth, I watched it slam into the rocks and disappear.

I looked back to shore. Waves were lapping over the rocks. I had to move forward, I couldn't go back. The next rock was just below the surface, and I saw that I'd have to get wet. Slowly, fearfully, I dropped down on my knees and crawled. The water swirled around me. I put out hands to the next rock. The rock fell away! I was up to my chest in the freezing, cold river.

I clawed at more rocks. They tumbled loose. The river tore at me, spun me around, swept me into the current. I screamed and swallowed water. My head went under; I came up choking. Tommy flashed through my mind.

No! Not me!

I was flung against something solid. I wrapped my arms around it, held on with all my strength. Coughing, gasping, fighting to keep my head above the water, I pulled myself along the fallen tree. Somehow—it seemed forever—I reached the roots, wedged in the rocks.

I flung myself down. I was on the opposite shore.

I was numb and shaking. My teeth were chattering. I tore off the freezing clothes stuck to my body.

I fell back, stared up into leafy branches.

My eyes closed.

The sun was gone. The bruises on my body were beginning to swell, and I ached all over. My clothes were nearly dry. I pulled them on. Barefoot, with nothing in the world, I limped upstream.

28
The Woods

The light grew dim. The woods were full of shadows. A thousand hidden creatures creaked and groaned. That stump. It couldn't be a wolf, could it? Those silent shapes—were they a whole pack of wolves?

I ran. I ducked behind trees, tripped over roots, fell—skinned my palms—and picked myself up and kept running. Did I hear yelps? Growls? Howls?

I saw a hollow tree, squeezed inside, and sank down in a mass of cobwebs. Squeaking mice ran out from under me. I heard only my own ragged gasps for breath.

Then a horrible shriek. An owl swooped past with something limp dangling from its claws.

My arms tight around my middle, I huddled in the tree and stared out at the dark.

I'm on the train. Running down the aisle. Jumping! Mrs. Krenkel is phoning the factory—then, suddenly, the night we'd left the city. Mrs. Krenkel standing on the stoop, her arms folded across her chest, watching my mother and me squeeze into the front seat of the hired truck. She's saying to my mother, "I have to hand it to you, Loretta. You do keep on."

The snapshot of my mother when she was a girl. My mother's hands twisting together. The lines on her face. Her job at that awful cannery. My mother standing by my door.

The soup. I made myself think about soup—the soup I'd make Beryl. I went through it step by step. First I'd light the stove and heat up the water. Then I'd cut up the vegetables and put them in the pot. I'd sprinkle in salt and pepper . . .

Above me the owl hooted. Shadows moved; underbrush crackled. Fiery red eyes stared in at me.

I sucked in my breath. I was alone. There was no one to help me.

I shut my eyes. Nothing moved. Not a sound.

I opened them.

Peering into the hollow tree were a couple of curious raccoons.

From somewhere, a faint rumble. A train's long, drawn-out whistle.

The raccoons shuffled into the shadows.

I let out my breath and leaned back.

. . . I'd add rice to make the soup thicker. . . .

29

Don

Daylight. I crawled out of the hollow tree and shivered in the cool air. I put my hand on the old, rough bark.

Then, a stab of fear. Where was I? I was all turned around.

Something shone through the trees. Light. Shimmery light. Light on water. I limped thankfully to the water's edge, soaked my cuts and sore feet, and knelt down to drink.

A dragonfly whirred past me, darted over the water, and zoomed upstream. I set out in the same direction.

The sun rose over the trees. The river turned from gray to blue. I trudged for hours, I could tell by the sun moving overhead. The river kept twisting and turning. Was I really sure? Was I really heading the right way? Yes. I had to be. I could tell by the current. I kept going.

The river became more like the river I knew, rippling between wide banks. I heard a horn, then a long whistle.

On the hill above me a train rumbled by. Was it only yesterday when I was on a train?

The rumbling faded. The river took another turn, wound around.

Suddenly I felt hot, then cold. My knees shook so hard I had to lean against a tree. Walt had said there were lots of rivers. What if this wasn't the right one?

I sank down on the ground. I had to calm myself, had to think. My head hurt.

I heard something, a grunt. Was it a bullfrog's grunt? Then, a tootle. It was a red-winged blackbird's song! I jumped up and ran through the trees.

Walt's marsh!

I couldn't believe it. I rubbed my eyes and looked again. A yellow butterfly drifted over. Giant green frogs sat in the mud. A mosquito whined and landed on my face. If I hadn't been so shaky, so tired, I'd have danced for joy.

I skirted around the muddy water, half expecting to see Walt, to hear his big voice, and I tried to smooth down my matted hair. Beryl and Walt would be on the porch, waiting for me. Oh, I was lucky. They'd help me, tell me what to do. There would be something good to eat from the garden. I could slurp up a whole watermelon on my own.

In the woods a blue jay squawked at me. A squirrel ran up and down a tree and chattered. At the KEEP OUT sign, I found the place where the barbed wire was loose and inched under.

The sky was blue and the sun was warm on my back. The cows all turned in a group and gazed at me.

I held up my head, ready to punch anyone who tried to stop me. I marched through Mr. Crain's beautiful clover and alfalfa field.

I was at Beryl's fence. I climbed over and walked around to the front of the house. The watermelons lay on the straw, big and dark green, ready to harvest.

But something was wrong. Don sat in the porch swing, leaning on his elbows, his head in his hands.

I went up the steps.

Don lifted his head. "Charley! They're searching for you! Thank God you're safe—your mother's beside herself—I locked up the store, told her I'd wait here in case you showed up—told her you'd most likely come here—"

He stopped. His face looked gray.

"Charley—" He moved over in the swing. "Sit down."

I looked through the screen door. "Where's Beryl?"

30
Mom

"**C**harley, we took Beryl to the hospital last night."

No.

"Beryl wanted me to tell you. She's giving you her—"

"I don't want anything!"

"Beryl's very sick." Don's voice was low. "We don't think—"

"No!" I yanked open the door and stumbled into the house.

The tomatoes I'd picked two days ago still lay on the sink.

"Beryl!"

No answer. She wasn't in the front room. Or in bed.

The teddy bear lay on the front-room sofa. I sank down and pressed it to my face.

Don came in and sat next to me.

I managed to ask, "Where's Walt?"

"Gone. Mr. Crain pressed charges. Walt had to leave

in a hurry." Don put his arm around me. "We'd better go to your mother. She was here, you know. After she heard you never got to the city she came here looking for you and found Beryl on the floor. She ran to get me, then held Beryl when I drove to the hospital. Your mother's back at your house now, waiting . . . . "

I held onto the teddy bear.

He got up. "Let's go home now, Charley."

I shook my head. Sweet Pea jumped into my arms and I held him, too.

"OK. But listen to me. I promise I'll take you to see Beryl later. But for now, stay right here. Don't move. I'll be right back. OK?"

I stared at my pictures on the wall and nodded.

Don's truck rattled off.

I wanted to run. I wanted to throw stones. I wanted to throw till I couldn't throw anymore. But I sat. Like a stone. A stone with a big hole in it.

The sun slanted through the window. It drifted across the wall and lit up a drawing of Sweet Pea. It shone on the frogs, then settled on the cows. I got up, went into Beryl's bedroom, and brought out my painting of her and Tommy and tacked it up with the others. The light rested on the cloud Beryl and the small cloud boy.

I heard Don's truck. The gate creaked open. Someone was running through the grass.

My mother burst into Beryl's front room.

"How could you–I pictured you . . ." Her face was swollen. "They found your suitcase–split open–in the river! I thought–Charlotte–oh my God. I thought you were dead!" She took a step.

I stood up. Was she going to hit me?

She covered her face and sobbed.

The light moved over my mother's shaking shoulders, her frazzled hair, her work-rough hands. Somehow she looked smaller, younger.

I can't stop crying. My baby doll is lost; she disappeared when Daddy, Mama, and I had to move again. I know she's gone forever. Dolly's blue nightgown that Mama made–and the blue, ruffly pillow–are gone, too. I'm in Mama's bed. She's holding me close–she's crying with me.

I felt that I was seeing my mother for the first time.

She sobbed as if her heart were breaking.

All of us poor, beautiful creatures, Beryl had said. Every butterfly. Every child. Every person.

I swallowed.

"Mom. . . ."

31
The Hospital

Don drove us to Amesville Hospital, told us where we could find Beryl, and said he'd wait. Inside the hospital was a suffocating smell, like all kinds of other bad odors were hiding under it. A sign said, Visiting Hours, 2:00 p.m. to 4:00 p.m. No Children Allowed.

We hung around till no one was in sight, then sneaked down the hall.

We peeked in the room. Six beds were lined up. The first five were filled with sleeping shapes covered with sheets. The sixth bed was empty. Beryl was propped in a chair by the window in a corner of sun.

A stern-faced nurse came up behind us. "Didn't you read the rules? No children can go in."

I wasn't sure I wanted to go in. Beryl looked so small and was sitting so still. But my mother said, "Please, Miss, we want to see Mrs. Stubbs. My daughter—just for a minute."

The nurse looked from my mother to me. "All right then," she said. "For a minute."

We tiptoed to the chair.

Beryl saw us. Her mouth curved up. Her eyes were blue pinpoints of light.

We knelt by her side.

"My watermelons . . ." Beryl's voice was a whisper. "A taste . . ."

I couldn't speak. My mother touched my hand.

"And Charley—and something else—my house—it's for you—yours—you and your ma—your home."

My home?

Beryl laughed weakly at our stupefied faces.

At first neither of us could believe it, couldn't seem to hear it. And when my mother finally *did* hear it, *did* understand that Beryl was giving us her house and land, she cried, and said, "I'd forgotten there were people like you in the world, Mrs. Stubbs."

I took Beryl's hand. It was almost transparent. Like a cocoon after the butterfly flies away. And, out of the blue, I remembered my lizard and butterfly dream, and the way the dream had ended with them planting the seeds.

"Time's up." The nurse was back.

"Beryl," I whispered, "I'll bring you some watermelon tomorrow."

Her eyes were on me, wouldn't let go.

The nurse shooed us away.

Outside the door, I looked back. Beryl's head was turned toward me.

I'll tell her that the slice of watermelon looks like a funny magenta-red smile. I'll tell her the lizard and butterfly dream.

And Beryl will laugh and say, "That's just how it is."

The next morning I sidestepped the nurse and ran to Beryl's room, with the slice of watermelon wrapped in waxed paper.

But Beryl's bed was empty. And her chair.

32

The Song

There was a breeze. The air was soft. Just as if it was the end of any ordinary August day.

Don and my mother were stooping over the hole, were sprinkling flowers on the nailed-down coffin.

I wanted to yell, "Beryl doesn't belong in there!" But I just stood, watching someone I didn't know shovel earth on top.

BERYL STUBBS, 1859–1936

Between Leon and Tommy.

Someone else I'd never seen before was saying, "The poor old soul is up in heaven now."

I looked up. Not a cloud in the pure blue sky.

No.

I looked back down at the mound of earth.

Maxine handed me a bunch of daisies. Mikey stood next to her. I hadn't noticed they were there.

The people I didn't know left. I kept my eyes on the bare mound.

"Charlotte," my mother said, "we'll keep it nice. And next spring we'll plant flowers."

I shook my head no.

I'll fill up the empty space with milkweed that the caterpillars eat, and clover and alfalfa for the butterflies. I'll plant watermelons—an apple tree—a peach tree . . .

The sun glowed low in the sky.

My mother touched my arm. "I think it's time to go."

I shook my head no. Not yet.

The sun sank behind the trees.

The mound of earth changed color, turned gold.

From behind a tree, I saw something move. The low light outlined a bald head fringed with white.

An old man, holding a battered, wide-brimmed hat. Walt.

He stepped out and nodded at me.

I nodded back.

Beryl loves to sing.

I've brought you a new song, Beryl . . .

The song started in my chest, rose up.

> This little light of mine,
> I'm gonna . . .

I didn't know who began to sing it out loud. If it was Walt. Or me. Mikey sang—and Maxine. And Don. Maybe even my mother.

The light turned deeper.

We sang it under the brilliant red sky.

Epilogue

The late October morning light is seeping into my room. At my feet, Sweet Pea is stretching, is opening his eyes, is closing them again. I slip out of bed, pull on a sweater and pants, and pick up my new sketchbook and box of crayons I earned by working at the store for Don after school. Don said he'd help me with the garden next year. And with planting a peach tree. Maybe an apple tree, too.

In the front room, Tommy's teddy bear is propped up on the sofa.

It's Sunday. My mother is still asleep.

On the porch I sit in Beryl's chair and rock back and forth. An empty cocoon is swinging on the vine. It's still showing the shape of wings.

I go down the porch steps and settle myself in the straw. A cold wind nips at my nose and my cheeks, but the garden is where I need to be. I curl the last green tendril of the watermelon vine around my finger. I hold the brown stem. And then I set to work.

On the first white page I draw the giant lizard in the darkness of space with the golden butterfly inside his head. I make sure to put in a sky-full of stars. On the second page I show the butterfly directing the lizard down through the sky to the tiny blue planet. I just get in its name: Planet Earth. On the third page they're on Earth planting seeds in the ground. Just like in my dream.

I keep going, make up the rest.

I draw the plants springing up and turning into people. A spreading watermelon vine becomes Beryl, and the biggest watermelon has Beryl's face, with the butterfly perched, like a bow, on top.

I stop and think. My mother had been like a puny, dry plant trying to grow through hard rocky soil. Now, planted next to Beryl on the page, she's a blooming orange squash flower.

Tommy is a tree full of ripe peaches. Don is a handsome corn stalk. I make a perky carrot look like Mikey, a pretty pink flower look like Maxine. I smile down at Walt. He's underground, a big red beet.

Walt is gone again. "I got ants in my pants, Charley," he'd said a few days after we buried her, "just like Beryl always told me. But" he'd tried to wink and grin at me, "just as sure as the butterflies and the lizards will be back—I'll be back, too."

I fill up all the empty places with green.

I study my picture. With my finger, I trace around the butterfly, and the lizard, and Beryl, and my mother, and every growing thing.

But I've left someone out.

I take a deep breath, choose blue crayon, and in the corner of the green, I draw a blue weedy flower—my dad.

The space inside of me is big enough to hold it all.

Last of all I draw myself. Sprouting up in the middle of everybody, and with my arms stretched out into all the colors.

And, at the bottom, in words like tiny new seeds, I write,

> "This picture is by me.
> Charlotte."